*Chi*ENERGY
WORKBOOK

*Chi*ENERGY
WORKBOOK

*a practical guide to the essence that
links all holistic therapies*

SIMON G. BROWN

STERLING PUBLISHING CO., INC.
NEW YORK

Published in 2004 by Sterling Publishing Co., Inc.
387 Park Avenue South
New York, NY 10016

First published in 2003 in the United Kingdom by
Carroll & Brown Publishers Limited
20 Lonsdale Road
London NW6 6RD

Project Editor Anna Amari-Parker
Managing Art Editor Emily Cook
Photographer Jules Selmes

Distributed in Canada by Sterling Publishing Company
c/o Canadian Manda Group
One Atlantic Avenue, Suite 105
Toronto, Ontario, Canada M6K 3E7

Reproduced by Colourscan in Singapore
Printed and bound by Tien Wah Press in Singapore

Sterling ISBN 1-4027-1701-6

CONTENTS

Foreword	6
What is chi energy?	8
Making chi energy work for you	10
How to use this book	12
Applying chi energy	14

EXPLORING *Chi* ENERGY   16

Principles of chi energy	18
Chi energy therapies	20
Chi energy toolbox	26
Internal chi boosters	28
External chi boosters	30
Accessing inner chi	32
Feeling another's chi	34
Feeling the chi from the ground	36
Shiatsu	*38*
Kinesiology	42
Using a pendulum to locate the chakras	44
Tuning in to someone else's thoughts and emotions	46

Chi ENERGY
AND THE MIND 48

Using your mind to change your chi 50

The first thought of the day 54

Food for clarity of thought 56

Teas to influence the mind 64

Body alignment 66

Freeing the chi of your mind 68

Tsubo therapy 70

Clearing your mental space 72

Expanding your mind 76

Feng shui 80

Promoting better sleep 84

Rituals before going to bed 86

Chi ENERGY
AND THE BODY 90

Using your mind to move chi
through your body 92

Moxibustion 96

Food for a beautiful and healthy body 98

Skin scrubbing 104

Clothing and colors 108

T'ai chi 112

Acupressure points for energy
and relaxation 118

Chi gong 122

Cupping 126

Chi ENERGY
AND THE EMOTIONS 128

Meridian stretches 130

Creating an atmosphere for
successful relationships 136

Reiki 140

Fine-tuning your chakras 144

Better sex by channeling chi
through the chakras 150

Eating to nourish your soul 154

Index 158

Acknowledgments 160

FOREWORD

I first encountered the idea of chi energy at the beginning of the 1980s when I embarked on a macrobiotic diet and the study of shiatsu massage techniques in my search for answers about the world that my engineering education could not provide.

I initially thought that chi energy was something unique to macrobiotics and shiatsu but, as the years went by, I discovered that chi energy principles underpinned all of the therapies I went on to learn about. Chi was the vital factor in feng shui, chakra calibration, reiki, meditation, acupressure, body alignment, meridian stretches, t'ai chi, chi gong, and moxibustion—all of which became part of my later professional life.

I loved the way that my study of chi energy was not purely intellectual or academic, but represented a real hands-on approach to healthy and happy living. The ancient Eastern concept of chi could be applied to any mind-body discipline, and I began to make the most incredible connections between myself and the surrounding world. With the help of Japanese mentors, I was able to feel, and eventually "see," this kind of energy. Over the years, my understanding of chi energy has developed to such an extent that I have used this knowledge to "invent" my own therapies for clients.

While running healing centers in both London and Philadelphia, I started to soak up more and more knowledge about chi energy. I sensed that it was the common thread running through everything, from why we behave differently during a full moon to how a rain cloud can influence our environment and moods. As a philosophical concept, chi energy helped make sense of everything but it was a little like mountain-climbing—just when I thought I had reached the final peak, yet another range spread out before my eyes. In the space of a few years of enquiry, more pieces of life's jigsaw have come together. I have come to realize that this puzzle is a lot bigger than I had at first anticipated, and I am still enjoying the challenge of getting the remaining pieces to fit.

In this book, I want to teach you a little about how this vital force works, and its applications to healing and wellbeing. Rather than treating the therapies in isolation, I would like to help you locate your chi, which you can then use to better yourself and others. Working with chi will provide you with a firm foundation for personal development, self-understanding, and a better quality of life.

The most interesting part of my work is the people I am privileged to treat. I cannot really say that I prefer to administer a shiatsu rather than give a feng shui consultation or perform moxibustion—it is the people with whom I interact that make what I do so worthwhile. My hope is that this book will empower you to really make the most of the rest of your life.

WHAT IS CHI ENERGY?

A subtle electromagnetic force permeates everything in the universe to sustain life and activity. It essentially connects us to everything else and is called chi or *qi* in China, *ki* in Japan, and *prana* in India. It permeates all matter and flows through all living things as it travels from one entity into another carrying information in much the same way that blood courses through your veins bringing nutrients to the various body parts. The human body is a complex field of continually moving chi circulating through cells, tissues, muscles, and internal organs.

In accordance with energy principles, chi cannot disappear nor can it be destroyed, but moves and changes from one form to another, and is easily replenished on a day-to-day basis. Imagine the flow of chi as a radiating energy "field" that runs through you and around you transporting thoughts, beliefs, and emotions, but mixing in with other dynamic influences around you as well. Some of this substance is continuously moving away from you as it comes to be replaced by other energy from your surroundings, rather like a magnetic field. Because humankind feels and thinks through life, there is a

ENERGY CIRCUITS
Chi is like a multi-lane superhighway of energy that picks up and carries information from one entity into another. It drives and links everything in the universe so that even the tiniest event light years away will eventually come to ripple through each one of us.

THE VARIOUS "FACES" OF CHI

For me, my understanding of my chi means that I can better assess my moods and, if I want to, find ways to change them. For example, if I feel low, I can choose foods with energy to bring my chi up, I can meditate or stretch in a way that frees my chi to move up my body, or visit places with an atmosphere that changes my chi in a way that makes me feel better. I can apply the same thinking when I am not feeling well, have challenges in life, or need a different perspective.

concentration of chi—also known as mass consciousness—encircling the planet. Everyone's ideas and thoughts surround us. If you are able to relax and tap into these "thoughts," you may pick up interesting insights and even solutions to your problems.

Allow the flow of chi to work for you: firstly, by understanding how it moves; and secondly, by applying it to the areas of your life that need it the most. The continuous exchange of chi between the inside and the outside is what effectively connects you to everything around you. The fresh chi that you draw in will bring in something of the surrounding world—aspects of the weather, the chi of people close to you, the atmosphere in your home, even the energy of what you eat. Such concentrations are often too small to be perceptible, but far more powerful chi forces, like the chi of the moon and of the weather, have noticeable effects on our behavior patterns. The make-up of your inner chi can be affected through the fabric of your clothes, the exercise you do, where you stand, and the activities that fill up your day. As different types of chi impact on your outer energy field, they will alter the composition of your inner chi and influence your thoughts and feelings.

MAKING CHI ENERGY WORK FOR YOU

Tap into the heart of the universal energy that is chi and use it to make powerful changes deep inside yourself. Different types of inner and outer chi connect you to the cosmos and everything in it. Inner chi circulates thoughts and feelings around your body and what you think and feel changes as it fluctuates and interacts with the outer chi from your surroundings. Learn to regulate chi and enjoy a healthier mind, body, and emotions.

Chi ENERGY AND THE MIND

Although we excel at developing our minds in conventional ways—linguistically, creatively, logically, spatially, socially, physically—we rarely develop our mental capacity to successfully channel chi. Some individuals, like paranormalists, are able to focus their mental energy so intently that they are able to move, and even change, the physical structure of objects (like bending metal spoons). Others, like clairvoyants and tarot readers, can tap into the energy field of another to reveal insights about that person. Kung fu practitioners rely on mental powers to perform feats of incredible skill and agility. There also have been cases of people who have found the strength to overcome terminal illness, or been able to triumph over adversity by adopting new belief systems. These kinds of phenomena testify to the mind's ability to focus and channel chi with profound results. My book contains ways to help you nourish and unleash this ability.

Chi ENERGY AND THE BODY

The majority of people tend to view their bodies as objects on which to "hang" clothes, as vehicles to carry their weight around, or as channels through which to perform vital functions. Individuals tend to take their bodies for granted and only "listen" to them when they start feeling aches and pains.

Your body is the "antenna" of your chi energy field. Stretching out your arm one way will pull your energy field in a certain direction. Even such a small gesture can subtly influence what you think and feel. Eastern practices like t'ai chi and yoga move and stretch chi in this way through a range of postures that encourage a more harmonious flow. The result is greater mental clarity, feelings of calm, and inner strength.

When chi is flowing freely, you radiate health and your skin, muscles, tendons, ligaments, blood vessels, internal organs, and bones retain their elasticity. Knotted muscles, hardened arteries, brittle bones, or dry skin are all signs your chi is disturbed and that its natural flow around the body has been obstructed. Test your skin's elasticity (see opposite) to gauge how well chi is flowing through you.

Chi ENERGY AND THE EMOTIONS

We are defined by our feelings which, along with our bodies and minds, complete our triangle of existence. When you are young, you tend to wear your heart on your sleeve but, as you get older, you exercise more control over what you feel. Yet, even as an adult, your inner chi is prone to changes as it interacts with outside energy. This quickly affects your emotions, which are changeable and susceptible to other influences: all it sometimes takes is for the sun to come out, for you to unexpectedly meet an old friend, or get out of the house to go for a walk.

Pent-up emotions cause problems because they contain trapped chi, so it is important to keep energy moving freely.

TEST YOUR SKIN'S ELASTICITY

The quality of your skin is evident from how elastic and supple it feels. Free-flowing chi and healthy skin go hand in hand.

1 Put your palms together. Begin to move them as far away from each other as possible, keeping your fingers together. If you can bend your palms to an angle of 90 degrees, you are in fantastic shape. Most people manage between 45-75 degrees.

2 Take a thin pinch of skin between thumb and forefinger from the top of your forearm. Pull the skin to test its elasticity.

3 Lie on your back and bend your knees. Bring your feet toward your buttocks. Push your right hand under your right rib to feel your liver. If there is resistance, the organ has hardened and is unhealthy.

HOW TO USE THIS BOOK

My Japanese mentors, Michio Kushi and George Ohsawa, used to encourage everyone who attended their classes to embrace setbacks, even hardships, as a pathway to becoming better and stronger people. My years of helping people overcome difficulties have taught me there is no magic cure for life's problems. Perhaps human development itself is dependent on rising to, and overcoming, a challenge. Your primary goal should be to develop the internal resources that you need to make the most of your life by learning the skills you need to be a more successful person. The idea is to break down the blockages and change patterns that have prevented success in the past.

This book draws on the chi energy practices that I have found helpful over the years—acupressure, reiki, shiatsu, t'ai chi, chi gong, cupping, feng shui, body alignment, moxibustion, meditation, breathing, meridian stretches, chakra calibration, and skin scrubbing. All can be incorporated easily into daily living, making this approach very powerful, regardless of whether you're working through physical or emotional problems.

There are four sections—exploring chi energy; chi energy and the mind; chi energy and the body; and chi energy and the emotions. Wherever your problem area lies—mind, body, or spirit—use at least one practice from each chapter for a more holistic approach. To alleviate a physical discomfort you could use acupressure on the body, meditation to help you to focus your chi energy on it, and chakra calibration to release negative emotions.

DIVINATION AND KINESIOLOGY

Adopt the process of divination to tap into your inner self and select the chi practices in this book that are ideal for you. Take a pack of playing cards and select 29 of them. Write down one of these numbers on the inside of each card: 38, 50, 54, 58, 62, 64, 68, 72, 76, 80, 84, 86, 92, 96, 100, 104, 108, 112, 116, 120, 124, 130, 132, 136, 140, 144, 146, 150, and 154. They all correspond with page numbers in the book. As you shuffle the cards, concentrate on something that you want to develop within yourself. Select a card. Turn it over, look at the number, and go to that page.

Alternatively use kinesiology exercises (see pages 42-43) and work with a partner. Get him/her to place the cards on your body, one at a time, and let him/her test your reaction. Have your partner place the cards on your forehead if you want to resolve mental issues; on your chest for emotional concerns; on your abdomen for physical ailments. Eliminate cards with little or no reaction. Focus on those that evoke a strong response. Do the activities suggested on those pages.

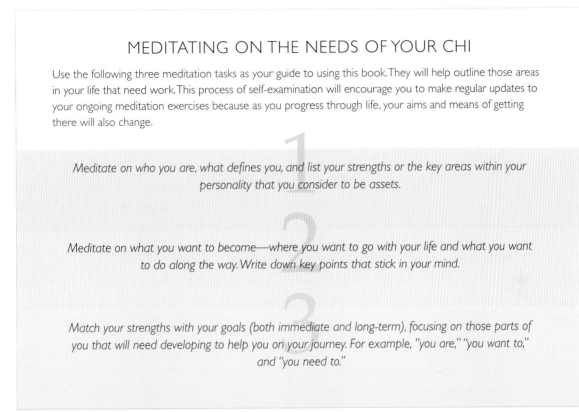

MEDITATING ON THE NEEDS OF YOUR CHI

Use the following three meditation tasks as your guide to using this book. They will help outline those areas in your life that need work. This process of self-examination will encourage you to make regular updates to your ongoing meditation exercises because as you progress through life, your aims and means of getting there will also change.

Meditate on who you are, what defines you, and list your strengths or the key areas within your personality that you consider to be assets.

Meditate on what you want to become—where you want to go with your life and what you want to do along the way. Write down key points that stick in your mind.

Match your strengths with your goals (both immediate and long-term), focusing on those parts of you that will need developing to help you on your journey. For example, "you are," "you want to," and "you need to."

The process set out above can help you choose certain kinds of activities over others as dictated by your needs and character traits. Bear in mind that the most obvious link might not necessarily be the most beneficial. A physical ailment may be cured by meditation, for example, or an emotional upset lessened by physical exercise. Work through this process of self-examination to customize this book specifically to you: firstly, meditate on what kind of results you would benefit from most; secondly, choose a set of activities, one from each chapter, which will aid you to achieve these goals. After a few weeks, review the effects of these activities on issues that concern you and note down any changes. If you are making headway, continue as you are. If there is little improvement, choose another combination of exercises from each of the chapters. Work these new practices into your life to bring about a newfound and effortless strength.

APPLYING CHI ENERGY

WORKING ON YOUR OWN
Chi gong liberates your movements and expands your capacity to work with the dynamics of chi.

Since chi energy underlies all things, applying any of these holistic practices to your life will produce results. Below, I discuss certain important areas—vitality and mental clarity; body and mind; relationships and sex—and describe which specific chi-boosting techniques are recommended and why.

Shiatsu, body alignment, t'ai chi, moxibustion, reiki, sexual bonding, and chakra calibration are techniques best done working with a friend or partner. If you prefer practicing alone, skin scrubbing, breathing exercises, meditation, and chi gong are ideal. I will cover these in detail later in the book.

VITALITY AND MENTAL CLARITY

Your ability to absorb chi energy from the outside world defines how much chi, and therefore vitality, you have. The food you eat, the way you breathe, restful sleep, acupressure, feng shui of the home, even the correct type of clothing, will all make a difference. Once you have absorbed fresh chi, it needs to be kept moving through regular skin scrubbing, meridian stretches, and shiatsu massage. To release deeper layers of stagnant chi, try working on your chakras, chanting, and meditation.

When the flow of chi is harmonious, it is easier to attain mental clarity. If your chi becomes turbulent, your thinking patterns will be fuzzy. Most of us experience this type of blockage in the form of stress. Conversely, when your chi is too dispersed, it becomes difficult to concentrate.

BODY AND MIND

Many physical aches and pains are caused by an excess or a deficiency of chi in a localized area. Because chi feeds into every living cell, it has a tremendous potential to heal; breathing techniques, coupled with positive imagery exercises, will suffuse your body with positive emotional energy. Shiatsu, moxibustion, acupressure, t'ai chi, chi gong, skin scrubbing, body alignment, and reiki all help to mobilize slow-moving energy around the body.

Facilitating the movement of chi energy encourages the release of painful feelings. Emotional hang-ups come from holding on to certain feelings for too long. Strong emotions, such as anger, depression, jealousy, fear, anxiety, and panic, can affect you positively by instigating drastic changes to your inner chi—

rather like a storm passing through the land, clearing the air and stirring things up. From time to time, such upheavals may be necessary. Come to see them as opportunities for self-improvement.

You also can absorb beneficial chi through what you eat. A diet high in unprocessed living foods like grains, beans, nuts, seeds, fresh vegetables, and fruit will naturally provide you with a healthier intake of chi.

RELATIONSHIPS AND SEX

Energy is continuously being shared, projected, and received between individuals. Social interaction can therefore be interpreted as the ebb and flow of chi between people that leads to the creation of societies and communities. If you have trouble forming or keeping friendships, you may want to learn to project your chi in ways that express your personality positively, and how to absorb other's energy harmoniously. Doing exercises in pairs, practicing t'ai chi, administering a shiatsu, or performing reiki are all methods for practicing this kind of interaction.

Partnerships between people often develop an energy of their own. Learning how to merge energy positively can generate healthier relationships. This relationship energy changes how you think, behave, and feel in the presence of your partner. Once dependencies, prejudices, and insecurities set in, they are hard to shake off, and obstruct the course of a happy relationship. Sometimes such negative energy is carried over from one relationship to the next and results in a pattern that repeats itself.

Passionate sex is a powerful method for merging another person's chi with your own and results in the exchange of some energy from both your respective energy fields. All your chakras will be activated and replenished with new chi. For a more satisfying sex life, try massage, chakra calibration through sexual bonding, meridian stretches, and applying feng shui techniques in the bedroom.

WORKING WITH A PARTNER
The motions of t'ai chi teach you to give and take as you both work toward a mutual benefit based on trust.

15

EXPLORING
Chi ENERGY

Chi energy emanates from everything in the universe and each individual's ability to harness it underpins Eastern therapies like feng shui, reiki, t'ai chi, shiatsu, chi gong, acupressure, and moxibustion. Understanding the essence and the mechanics of chi will enable you to regulate and manipulate this universal force to achieve mental, physical, and emotional balance. This chapter is all about discovery. Learn to access your inner chi, feel another's energy field, detect the chi emanating from the ground, locate the chakras, and tune in to someone else's thoughts and emotions. In addition, there is a special feature, where I will show you how to give a shiatsu massage.

PRINCIPLES OF CHI ENERGY

KIRLIAN PHOTOGRAPHY
This electrical imaging technique measures the concentration of life force (such as chi energy) in living organisms.

I believe that everything in the universe is permeated with and radiates chi energy. In 1937, the Russian scientist Semyon Kirlian (1900-1980) invented a photographic process that produced a halo-like outline around an object, rather like a multicolored gas flame. He believed this contour represented some sort of life force—effectively the object's chi energy field, which can change with surprising ease. Two people who are kissing passionately, for instance, will produce a very different energy field picture than when they are sitting quietly. This phenomena extends into the natural world as well. You can pull a leaf off a plant and, using the Kirlian method, photograph the empty space that the leaf formerly occupied to see the outline of its shape.

No longer such a narrow ideology, science is becoming increasingly accepting of a world with no fixed answers. Modern scientists can never declare anything to be "for sure," but can only calculate the probability of something happening. Our world is not as black and white as we once thought and the ancients picked up on this uncertainty to develop fluid philosophies. As more scientific discoveries are made, some of these theories, like chi, are shown to be surprisingly relevant.

PERSONAL CHI ENERGY
To my mind, your inner and outer chi energy collectively make up your "aura," a discernible, halo-like emanation around your body that manifests as a glow of various colors to reflect the subtle life energies within. This is the way that you interact intuitively with the world around you and is sometimes referred to as your sixth sense.

DIFFERENT TYPES OF CHI ENERGY

The chi energy within and around you possesses changing characteristics and can therefore influence the way you think and feel in particular ways at specific times. Surrounding chi is always in a state of flux, as it moves from day to night, through the seasons, and into different weather conditions. Similarly heartbeat and breath affects the way in which your internal chi energy flows. Your inner chi and external chi energy also influence each other as they go through their cycles.

Compressed/dispersed

When chi becomes compressed or "trapped" in certain parts of the body, the affected areas feel tense, or tight. You could, for example, have a headache that makes your head feel like it's about to explode. We are prone to experiencing compressed chi when there is high air pressure or when we feel stressed, angry, and irritable.

When your chi is too dispersed, it results in feelings of emptiness or apathy. You'll struggle to get warm and feel that your legs are weak. When your life energy is dissipating, you can feel depressed, emotionally drained, and exhausted. People with dispersed chi have lower inner chi levels and therefore seek energy from others.

Fast and turbulent/slow and stagnant

Chi energy can move quickly, and emotionally it may feel like you're caught in the middle of a thunderstorm. You will find it easier to overcome a trying emotional patch if you can speed up the movement of chi and "blow away" negative emotional energy. Excess fast-flowing chi, however, makes it difficult to feel inwardly settled.

When your chi moves slowly, it is easier to feel calm, an inner state more conducive to activities like meditation and self-analysis. If your chi energy moves too slowly, however, it will stagnate, making it harder to let go of lingering feelings. You can also become stuck in a rut if your connection with the world around you diminishes.

Ascending/descending

Chi rises more strongly through the body in the morning and particularly during springtime. This helps you feel uplifted, enthusiastic, and confident. But too much results in all talk and no action.

Chi levels tend to come down in the afternoon and during the fall. This makes it easier for you to feel settled, practical, and down-to-earth as your chi is drawn to the earth. A surplus of it could make you less adventurous.

Projecting, radiant, and outward/withdrawn, hidden, and inward

At times of intense emotion, or when you fly off the handle, your inner chi radiates outwardly to strongly project what you're feeling. In excess, though, it can make you come across as arrogant and overbearing.

When you want to generate internal focus and strength, draw chi inwardly to feel a deeper power. If you do this excessively, you risk cutting yourself off from the world and the surrounding energies that keep you balanced.

CHI ENERGY THERAPIES

THE CROWN CHAKRA (SAHASRARA)

THE MIDBRAIN CHAKRA (AJJNA)

THE THROAT CHAKRA (VISHUDDHI)

THE HEART CHAKRA (ANHATA)

THE STOMACH CHAKRA (NABHI)

THE ABDOMEN CHAKRA (SWADISTHAN)

THE SEX CHAKRA (MOOLADHARA)

Over the thousands of years that the concept of chi energy has been in use in the East, different therapies have evolved. Although chi goes by different names, depending on the origin of the practice, all these Eastern therapeutic approaches are fundamentally underpinned by the same idea. The methods and disciplines that I will introduce represent well-established ways of manipulating and controlling your chi. Some, like t'ai chi, chi gong, breathwork, meditation, and feng shui, you can do yourself; others, like shiatsu, reiki, and body alignment, require a partner.

YOGA AND CHAKRA CALIBRATION

Originally from India, yoga is one of the oldest, best-known physical and mental practices for wellbeing. It coordinates breathing techniques, movement, and meditation to powerfully channel chi. The calibration of the body's seven energy centers—the chakras—is fundamental to the practice. From the Crown Chakra on the top of your head, which can become charged with energy from the heavens, to the Sex Chakra, designed to receive energy from the earth below, chi energy needs to be in balance along this "path." In ancient times, yogis believed that they could shift the directional flow of the chi in their chakras by inverting the posture of their bodies. Consequently, they developed sequences of stretches and body postures (or *asanas*) that increased elasticity and flexibility in different parts, which was important for overall physical health, by promoting the unrestricted flow of energy. These stretches and postures are extremely effective when combined with the correct meditation and breathing techniques. All grant greater mental clarity by activating free-flowing chi through the channels of the body.

THE ENERGY PATH OF THE CHAKRAS
Standing or sitting with your chakras lined up vertically makes it easier for chi to flow through them. Use a mirror to help you find the correct posture.

CAN ANYONE DO IT?

Everyone possesses chi energy and the potential to heal him- or herself and others. There is no monopoly or exclusive access to this vital life force. Exchanging chi energy with your practitioner during a therapy session should feel more like having a good talk with an understanding friend than paying a complete stranger who happens to be trained and qualified in the particular discipline that you are seeking to benefit from. In our day and age, what is essentially just a natural exchange between two people is dressed up as something complicated and expensive that requires years of training. This is in part brought about by pressures from the government for practitioners to be self-certified, partly to provide some kind of protection to the uninformed members of the public, and partly to create yet another business out of training people.

You may find that, having experimented with some of the self-help methods presented in this book, you then require the assistance of someone who is more experienced than you. In my opinion, you should seek professional help only if you have a serious problem.

All of these approaches are relatively well-known in the West now, so you should find it fairly easy to locate a practitioner through the internet, a local directory, or an accredited society. If you are concerned about verifying his/her credentials, find out whether he/she is a registered member of a professional organization, can produce reliable training certificates, and offer insurance. As strong changes to your chi require trust and confidence, it is helpful to meet him/her to see if you feel comfortable in his/her presence, and are willing to proceed with the treatment.

All the therapies in this book are subject to little or no cost and, in some cases, little training. My techniques are simple, safe to use, and are meant to be integrated into your everyday routine as part of a healthier, more natural lifestyle. Don't be put off by the more complex subjects such as acupressure, shiatsu, or feng shui, as there are always simpler aspects that anyone can attempt on his/her own or with a partner.

ACUPRESSURE

An ancient healing art developed in Asia over 5,000 years ago, acupressurists use fingers and thumbs, or perform moxibustion (a form of heat therapy which burns compressed moxa herb sticks), to stimulate key points on the surface of the patient's skin. The healing touch of acupressure boosts the body's self-curative abilities, relieving pain, reducing tension, promoting relaxation, rebalancing the body, and maintaining good health.

Like acupuncture, acupressure is based on the idea that, as energy flows through the various body meridians, of which there are 14, the quality of the local chi along their length can be changed by pressing into key points called *tsubos* to calm or stimulate the energy inside a whole meridian.

Acupuncture and acupressure use the same points, but acupuncture employs needles, whereas in acupressure, you use your thumbs or other parts of your body. This makes acupressure somewhat more personal and intimate. Each acupressure point will feed back information on the state of the receiver's chi and help to shape the treatment.

SHIATSU

In this, the most well-known style of acupressure, the practitioner uses his/her own body to feed or calm chi inside a patient through a combination of stretches, massage techniques, joint manipulation, pounding, rubbing, and the stimulation of acupressure points. Shiatsu is a very personalized form of treatment—the practitioner works closely with the patient to identify his/her limitations as a receiver during the treatment. It is extremely flexible, both in

acupressure

body alignment

shiatsu

feng shui

terms of the techniques used and the problem areas addressed. Techniques can be adjusted to be very gentle by incorporating the principles of reiki, for example, or be really quite vigorous.

When receiving shiatsu, the patient lies on a futon fully clothed (loose cotton clothing works best). A partial shiatsu is given using a stool or a chair. It is also possible to perform aspects of shiatsu, known as *do in*, on yourself.

BODY ALIGNMENT

The wear-and-tear of daily life causes parts of your body to tense up. Over time, such pressure can pull your body out of alignment, leading to increased stresses and strains on your muscles as they try to compensate for this shift. Body alignment represents a simple way of correcting your body's posture. As the patient lies on the floor, a trained expert checks whether reference points, such as his/her ankles and wrists, line up correctly. When an imbalance is found, gentle pressure is applied to specific points which triggers off waves of expanding chi. Tension is thus released from the side of the body being treated. It is important to ensure that a patient is correctly positioned before starting deeper work on his/her chi. Body alignment often provokes changes in breathing patterns and can even precipitate a liberating muscular spasm.

FENG SHUI

The Chinese art of geomancy revolves around creating the most harmonious and balanced atmosphere possible to allow you to live up to your full potential for success in life. Its essence is based on the idea of how the energy of your surroundings interacts with your personal chi to change the way you think and feel.

At the heart of feng shui practice is the belief that the highest concentration of chi is absorbed through the spiral at the top of your head (the Crown Chakra). The direction that it faces during sleep at night will significantly influence your chi energy field in the morning, as you will have absorbed a greater concentration of the chi from that direction. For example, sleeping with the top of your head pointing East helps you to absorb more of this uplifting morning and springtime energy. The same principle applies to the direction you face when seated.

Spending time in an atmosphere with the "right" kind of vibes helps to maintain good health, restore emotional balance, and sustain high energy levels. It is possible to change the quality and flow of the chi that moves through your living space by using colors, materials, and shapes to influence it. Much of the fine-tuning in feng shui is achieved by placing elements that you would find in your body (i.e. water, salt, and iron) in strategic places within your living or workspace. Feng shui tips are safe and easy to apply. If you want to treat a specific problem, however, you may want to consult a feng shui expert.

T'AI CHI

This martial discipline teaches you how to use an opponent's force to your advantage. A t'ai chi master will be able to push someone over with minimal physical contact by manipulating his/her adversary's chi energy. Considered the highest form of self-defence, it takes considerably longer to attain a level of proficiency in t'ai chi than in any other martial art.

Two fundamental principles underlie the art of t'ai chi. Firstly, the mastery of a sequence of movements that encourage a freer, more harmonious flow of chi through your body. To help this, you will need to increase the chi flow between your hands and that from the ground. Secondly, using your chi to interact with that of another person and acquiring an awareness of his/her chi, which you can then turn to your advantage.

CHI GONG

Similar to t'ai chi, chi gong is a Chinese approach to building and balancing the flow of chi through physical exercises, internal meditation, and concentration. It helps the body create its own subconscious muscular responses for healing, wellbeing, fitness, and longevity. Chi gong trains the mind to direct movement toward those body parts where chi energy is trapped, or is stagnating, and release it. Initially you may find it easier to work with a master, who can relax you and open up your outer chi energy field—the starting point from which to begin working on the movements. These stretches and postures mimic naturally occurring aspects of nature and use the Chinese principle of the Five Elements (water, wood, fire, earth, and metal) to redress physical or emotional imbalances.

reiki

t'ai chi

chi gong

REIKI

Chi energy blockages are often at the root of physical pain—when they are lifted, more energy can enter chi-deficient areas and emotional balance is restored. Originally developed in Japan, reiki makes use of the hands as tools for healing. The reiki practitioner places his/her hands on different parts of another's body and holds them in position until the palms start to warm up, a sign that chi is effectively being redirected into the recipient. This process balances and enhances both the giver's, and the receiver's, chi flow.

Reiki training takes the giver through a purification process first to ensure that he/she will feed the receiver healthy chi. You can practice doing reiki with a friend on a regular basis as it's not time-consuming and very simple to do. Personally, I incorporate reiki into other healing treatments in order to make powerful connections with the chi of my patients. After the sessions are finished, my clients say that they continue to feel the presence of my hands for some time.

CHI ENERGY TOOLBOX

To me, good health means bringing the components of your internal world (body, mind, and emotions) into balance with your surroundings. Chi flow is bi-directional; it can be changed from the inside and the outside.

FROM THE INSIDE

BREATHING

You draw in fresh chi with every in-breath and expel old chi with every out-breath. Breathing represents a primal way of interacting with the chi energy around you and is one of the body's natural rhythms. How you breathe defines the quality of your interaction with this surrounding energy. If you do not breathe fully, you risk depression and lethargy.

MEDITATION / VISUALIZATION

This ancient method of relaxation stills the mind as you concentrate on a single word, phrase, or object. It enhances mental and spiritual development, encourages contemplation, and teaches how to direct inner chi to calm the turbulence of emotions, heighten spiritual awareness, and develop the powers of concentration. Visualization is the same except that you focus on an internal image.

TEAS

For thousands of years, drinking tea has been used as a method of healing and detoxifying (see pages 64-65). It brings specific types of chi energy deep into your body. Hot liquids contain far more energy and radiate out quickly producing a more dramatic effect than cold liquids.

FOOD

Of all the ways that chi energy can enter your body, you have the greatest control over the food that you eat and the kind of chi with which different ingredients are associated (see pages 56-63). Wild salmon that has swum upstream, for example, will possess a far greater concentration of fast, determined chi than a slow-moving squid that floats in warmer, calmer waters.

CHAKRAS

Locate these seven energy centers by dangling a metal ring from the end of a piece of thread over a person's body (see pages 44-45). Once it detects the spiraling chi activity of a chakra, the ring will begin to circle. Use chanting, palm healing, breathing, and meditation to enhance the way that your chi flows through and radiates out from your chakras.

FROM THE OUTSIDE

Similar to shiatsu, this system of healing concentrates on using the 360 acupressure points dotted along the 14 body meridians (see pages 70-71) to treat pain and discomfort. Each *tsubo*, or pressure point, represents a gateway into individual meridians. These points can be used to treat common ailments through their symptoms or as a means of raising overall chi energy levels.

MOXIBUSTION

In Traditional Chinese Medicine (TCM), the herb mugwort is administered as a moxa preparation and applied either as sticks or patches (see pages 96-97) to heat chosen acupressure points. This process of controlled combustion (since moxa does not burn with a flame but simply smolders) brings more energy into the meridians through the *tsubos* and is often used in conjunction with shiatsu. It is also effective for increasing the chi in a meridian to combat coldness or lack of energy.

SKIN SCRUBBING

Encourage a renewed flow of chi through your skin by stimulating blood circulation using a towel (see pages 104-107). This action has the added benefit of prompting the action of toxin-releasing pores that cleanse and regenerate the skin's four layers—the keratin layer, epidermis, dermis, and subcutaneous tissue. The lack of chemical soaps and detergents in scrubbing makes it the perfect all-round beauty regime that avoids upsetting your skin's delicate pH balance.

ENVIRONMENT

Beneficial chi can also be absorbed through your environment. All you have to do is put yourself in situations where the energy suits your needs. Sitting alone in a large cathedral, for example, generates a free-thinking energy while sitting in a small, crowded café can help you feel more practical. Surround yourself with people, locations, and objects that give off the kind of chi that you feel you either lack, need more of, or simply enjoy experiencing.

PEOPLE

Those around you inevitably project their own chi energy fields into the world. If you happen to be in close proximity to others, their energies will interact with, and impact on, your inner chi. If your chi energy is low, you would benefit from being near someone who is lively, outgoing, and boisterous. At times of great emotional difficulty, you might feel better being physically close to someone with positive, reassuring, and supportive chi energy.

INTERNAL CHI BOOSTERS

I've found that these internal chi boosters free up chi flow from within: breathing is a process of energy exchange; meditation and visualization invigorate you through mental images; once ingested, the chi in teas and food becomes part of the body's make up; all these work on your body changing your chi from within.

BREATHING

Close your eyes as you work through these different breathing relaxation techniques. Concentrate on inhaling through your nose and exhaling from your mouth.

Full breathing Sit or kneel and place your hand over your navel. Breathe in and expand your abdominal cavity so that it pushes your hand out. Breathe out. Once you are comfortable breathing into your abdomen, continue filling your chest. Forcefully exhale all the air from your body until you find a comfortable rhythm.

Energizing breathing Breathe in quickly and fully for two seconds, hold it in for one second, and breathe out fully for one second. Let out the sound "hugh" on the out-breath. Repeat several times until you feel energized. You might feel dizzy after a few breaths so sit on a chair or kneel on the floor. Stop if you feel light-headed.

Calming breathing Breathe in slowly for about six seconds. Hold your breath for four seconds. Breathe out slowly for at least six seconds.

MEDITATION / VISUALIZATION

Find a clean and relaxed space where you can sit in silence without fear of being interrupted. Place a lit candle before you as a focal gazing point. Stare at it and fix all of your attention into the sensation of each breath as it enters and leaves your body through the nostrils, mouth, throat, and lungs. Once your mind is completely focused on the rhythm of your breathing alone, begin to direct your train of thought elsewhere.

Begin by doing a slow, calming breathing exercise. With every in-breath, imagine you are drawing energy in from all around. Visualize breathing in a particular color, sound, or feeling and focus on a particular part of your body. Picture it turning the hue you've captured in your mind's eye. With every out-breath, capture your breath filling up a small part of the room at first, then gradually expand it to encompass the universe.

Teas are renowned as natural, quick-fix remedies for anything from digestive disorders to headaches. Hot liquids are quickly absorbed into the bloodstream and have a soothing effect on the digestive system. As water is the main ingredient in teas, and because our bodies are largely composed of water, the energy in tea interacts quickly and directly with the chi of the water inside us. For this reason, teas can impact both on long-term health and exercise a rapid influence on our emotions. Although there is a vast range of herbal teas available from health food stores and supermarkets, your chi will benefit more from a personalized concoction than a product that has been commercially pre-packaged.

Before making a particular brew, consider what kind of chi movement would help you most. If you have a thundering headache at the front of your head, for example, it would make sense to prepare an infusion with ingredients that help pull chi flow away from your temples. Conversely, if you were shivering, or feeling cold and tired, you would opt for ingredients to help draw in and retain energy.

Apart from following a diet that is nutritious and well-balanced, there are great benefits to be had from being aware of the kind of chi in different types of food. Everything you eat has its own chi energy field which, once inside you, will exert a subtle influence on your inner chi. If you continue to eat the same type of food over a long period of time, this will have a pronounced effect on the make up of your chi. Whole grains, dried beans, vegetables, fruits, nuts, and seeds are more "neutral" foods and make it easier to gauge fluctuations in your chi.

To learn more about the chi in food, think about how different things grow. Root vegetables (like carrots, onions, potatoes), for example, need strength to grow deep in the ground, whereas vegetables that grow above the soil (like squash or zucchini) have a more relaxed energy. Also consider the methods of preparation for different foods. Frying food on a high flame will add lots of fiery energy to ingredients while slowly stewing a dish will impart a slower kind of chi.

These areas of intense chi activity are situated at the top of your head (the Crown Chakra); between your eyebrows (the Midbrain Chakra); in your throat (the Throat Chakra); in the middle of your chest (the Heart Chakra); in your solar plexus (the Stomach Chakra); two finger-widths below your navel (the Abdominal Chakra or *hara*); and in your genital area (the Sex Chakra).

Each chakra relates to different emotions and aspects of human nature. The Crown Chakra processes energy connected with spirituality; the Midbrain Chakra controls the intellect; the Throat Chakra focuses on communication; the Heart Chakra manages the emotions; the Stomach Chakra guides ambition, motivation, and drive; the Abdominal Chakra is linked to vitality levels; the Sex Chakra dominates sexuality.

Use your hands to transmit energy and increase the flow of chi within individual chakras. Alternatively, use chanting and breathing techniques to send waves of chi to specific chakras, or channel energy into each one through meditation.

EXTERNAL CHI BOOSTERS

In my experience, certain actions or external influences promote the flow of chi through the skin: acupressure mobilizes chi through pressure points; moxibustion introduces heat and stimulates circulation; scrubbing draws blood to the body's surface and renews stagnant chi; even your environment and other people can affect the quality of your internal chi.

ACUPRESSURE

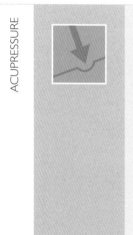

You can buy specialist anatomical charts that map out the tiny pressure point gateways to the body's large meridian chi channels. Life-like, color-coded figures with the meridians and acupressure points drawn on are also readily available. Both the anatomical charts and the figures come with tips on how to find and activate different *tsubos*. This book covers those acupressure points that are useful for treating common ailments and are easy to find.

To carry out acupressure on a particular point, draw in a deep breath and imagine you are sucking chi into the boundary of your energy field. Press your thumb into the *tsubo* as you breathe out and imagine that you are inwardly channeling chi. Repeat this technique several times before moving on to another point. Some *tsubos* may even be stimulated simply by rubbing.

MOXIBUSTION

Another method of working on acupressure points is to heat them up using either moxa sticks (large cigar-like sticks made from the herb mugwort) or self-adhesive patches. To use a patch, peel off the backing paper, and stick it over the appropriate point. As the herb smoulders, you will feel warmth spreading into the targeted area. If the heat is overpowering, pull the patch off immediately.

To use a moxa stick, first locate where you want to add more chi in the form of heat. Light one end and circle it over the acupressure point (or desired area) holding the stick above

your skin to ensure you don't burn yourself. When the level of heat starts to become uncomfortable, move the stick away until this sensation dies down, then continue. If skin reddens, this is often a sign that you have completed the treatment. Keep a bowl of water by your side to safely put out any burning sticks at the end of the session.

In Eastern medicine, your skin is considered to be the fabric that defines you both internally and externally. Before the air that you breathe in can properly become part of you, it must pass the body's first barrier—the lining of your lungs. Similarly food only enters after getting through the lining of your intestines. Therefore, if you want to improve the condition of your lungs or intestines, you can also work on your skin from the outside.

Skin scrubbing draws blood to the surface, promotes a renewed flow of chi, regulates metabolism, and creates a stronger link between your inner and outer chi. Stimulating your skin in this way spreads chi out more evenly. Scrub your skin early in the morning to feel refreshed and active; do it before going bed at night to relax you and help you get a good night's sleep. Scrubbing with hot water cleanses skin deeply as it pumps pores clean of clogging dirt. This ancient practice is all-natural and avoids tipping over the skin's delicate pH balance with the use of detergents.

Wherever you were born, whatever country you work or live in, whatever destinations you choose to visit on your vacations, you can't help but take in some of their ambient chi energy concentration.

The more time you spend in a given location, the greater the "pull" this place will have, so places where you live and work exercise a great deal of influence. Having said this, however, you also can find and visit inspiring places, which supply you with special types of chi energy at particular times, and you do not have to live in a large city to find them. Places like the Pantheon in Rome, the Frick Museum in New York, or a thatched cottage by a river do it for me. Whenever life seems difficult, going to your "secret hideaway" changes your perspective, renewing your chi.

In the outside world, every individual projects his or her own chi energy field. When these merge with your chi, slight changes begin to take place. Because such fusions can ultimately set off positive or negative reactions that affect us, it is important to surround ourselves with special people and be that special person in the lives of others.

We all need a good support network of people who can step in and change the way we think and feel when things go wrong. Sometimes just sitting next to someone is enough. You do not always need to say something. If you feel awkward about making physical contact at emotional times, you may find that giving someone a massage helps to break the ice. When feeling low, seek someone you can trust to confide in; someone who feels good to be around and that you feel comfortable exchanging chi with.

ACCESSING INNER CHI

MEDITATION /
VISUALIZATION

Being able to find and direct your chi gives you a wonderful feeling and a new sense of power. The simplest way to effectively make contact with and project chi is through your hands although, with practice, you could use any part of the body. My suggestion would be to find a peaceful location free from electrical equipment, clutter, and synthetic materials. Ideally this space should be reasonably large and could even be outdoors. Wear loose cotton clothing, so that your body feels unrestricted when moving, and select a time of the day when you are least likely to be interrupted. For optimal results, perform these exercises at sunrise while standing barefoot outside in the open air where you can feed off the fresh chi from the atmosphere.

GENERATING CHI

1 Vigorously rub the palms, backs, and sides of your hands together. Stroke the outside of your upper arms. Step forward with your right foot. Breathe in. On the exhale, stretch your hands up. Step back. Drop your arms. Step with your left foot. Repeat 3 times. Energetically shake your hands, keeping fingers and wrists relaxed.

2 Hold the base of your right thumb between your left thumb and index finger. Massage down to your thumbnail. Press at each side of the nail base as you breathe in. On the exhale, quickly pull away thumb and index finger. Visualize extending the edges of a multi-colored flame around your thumb. Repeat with all fingers.

ROUTES TO FINDING CHI

In my opinion, there are several routes you can follow to try to find and increase the intake of chi in your life. Make a concerted effort to eat foods high in "living" chi like fresh fruit, vegetables, beans, grains, nuts, and seeds. Whenever possible, wear clothing made of cotton or other natural fibers. Keep electrical equipment at a safe distance while you work, relax, or sleep. Choose bedding made from 100 percent pure cotton and ensure your home contains as many natural materials in it as possible. Perform meridian stretches on a weekly basis in an appropriately natural, well-ventilated environment. Practice t'ai chi, chi gong, or yoga regularly. Scrub your skin regularly. Carry out the chi meditation exercises that I've recommended below on a daily basis.

3 Put your palms together in front of your chest or neck. With every in-breath, imagine you are deeply breathing in a powerful color, sensation, or sound into a part of your body (i.e. the abdomen)—for example, a strong red heat or a lion's roar. With every out-breath, imagine the same color, feeling, or sound moving up into your hands. Repeat 12 times.

■ **SIMON'S TIP**
Sensing chi in or between your hands involves being able to detect a slight magnetic sensation or one of warmth. If you struggled with perceiving the presence of chi, regular practice will increase sensitivity.

4 Vigorously rub your palms together. Slowly move your hands closer and further apart. Feel the palms gradually warming up as your hands move closer; feel them start to pull this field of warm chi apart as you move them further away. Start slowly, gradually getting faster. Use small, then increasingly larger, distances. Close your eyes. Focus on the magnetic or warm sensation between your hands.

FEELING ANOTHER'S CHI

PEOPLE

In my experience, you can improve how you well you relate to others by developing your ability to sense and interpret their chi. The better you can do this, the more effortless your connection will be with other people. I believe that becoming more sensitive to sources of chi outside yourself maximizes your chances of obtaining accurate readings of people, forming healthy relationships, and avoiding unhealthy ones. This connection is most helpful with people already close to you like lovers or family members. Begin the techniques below with the chi-generating exercise on pages 32-33.

STANDING UP

1 Do this exercise in a room where you can both move about freely. Ask your partner to face away from you. Take 3-4 steps back. Hold out your arms, palms facing your partner's back, and move forward. Ask when he/she starts to feel anything.

2 Slowly move your hands toward and away from your partner. Detect whether there is any energy present between your hands and his/her back by coming forward to check whether this slight magnetic sensation becomes stronger. If you cannot feel anything, inch forward with your hands almost touching your partner's back for a stronger connection. Do this as silently as possible.

3 When it's your partner's turn to try to make contact with you from behind, try to relax. Concentrate on your breathing as you empty your mind, remaining only aware of your back and how it feels. With practice, you can learn to make your partner sway back and forth without making physical contact.

LYING DOWN

1 Ask your your partner to lie comfortably on his/her front on the floor, a towel, cushions, or a firm bed. Choose a space that is quiet and distraction-free.

2 Make sure you feel calm and relaxed before you begin. Kneel or sit next to your partner. Choose which hand you are going to use. Keep the other relaxed in your lap.

3 Run your hand over and above your partner's back to detect those parts giving off the most heat—areas with excess chi. Those that feel cold indicate chi deficiency. Hover your hand above and breathe chi into these areas. Once your palm

warms up, raise and lower your hand over your partner's back to test for the magnetic pull of chi. Measure the strength and extent of your partner's energy field by seeing how far you can raise your hand before you lose the connection. Eventually move your hand away.

4 When it's your partner's turn, sense the location of his/her hand and register any areas of localized warmth. Try to detect when his/her hand is moved away.

SITTING BACK-TO-BACK
Sit with your backs touching, but don't rest on each other. Assess whether any areas of your back feel warmer or cooler. Connect with your partner's breathing and the state of his/her back.

FEELING THE CHI FROM THE GROUND

ENVIRONMENT

As the Earth rotates, it expels chi. This energy rises deep from within the Earth's core and radiates out into the atmosphere, into the seas and lakes, soil and vegetation, atmosphere, and through buildings. Human beings live in contact with the Earth's surface and become like small "mobile antennae" for the chi leaving our planet. I believe it is important to spend time in touch with nature. These are essential moments for renewing our vital connection with the earth. These next two exercises are best done outside in a park or a garden in direct contact with the soil, preferably barefoot. Becoming aware of the energy from the ground lets you directly tap into a major source of chi.

WITH YOUR HANDS

1 Begin by doing the chi-generating exercise on pages 32-33. Stand with your feet shoulder-width apart. Spread out your toes. Relax your shoulders and let your arms flop down by your sides.

2 Bend your knees slightly as you lift your forearms as though a piece of thread were tied to your wrists. Keep your hands relaxed. Raise them, straighten your knees a little, and slowly breathe in. Focus on feeling the chi between your hands and the ground as a magnetic pull between your palms and the earth.

3 As you breathe out, gradually bring your hands back down to your sides as you straighten your knees. As you move your hands down, flex your wrists so your hands remain parallel to the ground.

WITH YOUR FEET

1 With your left foot firmly on the ground, slowly move your right foot forward and drop the heel until it makes contact with the earth. Feel your left foot firmly gripping it. Focus on the soles of your feet. Ask yourself questions about your initial contact with the earth: was it soft, hard, warm, cold, damp, dry, sharp, sandy, or wet?

2 Slowly roll your right foot forward so that the ball of the foot eventually touches the ground. Your body weight should still primarily be on your left foot. Once the right foot is firmly placed, start to move your weight forward and onto it. Concentrate on taking it off your left foot and, as it moves forward, let it overtake the right foot. Repeat. The slower the walk, the more difficult and beneficial it becomes. Focus on feeling every minute detail as your feet touch the ground in slow motion. If this is difficult, hold onto another person or against wall.

■ SIMON'S TIP

The secret to performing this exercise correctly involves keeping your hands and wrists relaxed. With practice, you will easily be able to coordinate your movements and your breathing.

SHIATSU

Shiatsu is an ancient healing art originating in Japan, which relies on the healing power of touch and pressure to keep the body healthy and flexible and the mind calm and relaxed. During a shiatsu session, the practitioner applies pressure with his/her thumbs, hands, elbows, knees, and feet to induce deep relaxation and well-being in the recipient. The techniques for giving a shiatsu are sometimes more dynamic or static, involving pressure, pounding, stretching, manipulation, and kneading.

In my experience of giving a shiatsu, you allow someone's else body rhythm to guide your own movements. It is important to establish a pattern and avoid sudden, jerky gestures. Rhythmically move your weight back and forth over your partner, applying pressure through your hands gradually and slowly. Combine this with long, powerful out-breaths and a positive projection of chi.

CONTROLLING PRESSURE AND BREATHING

During shiatsu, you must tune in to and match your partner's breathing pattern like a form of moving meditation between giver and receiver that is beneficial to both of you. I suggest that you begin a shiatsu massage session by resting your hand on your partner's back or abdomen to follow the rhythm of his/her breathing.

You can apply pressure with any part of your body, but it comes most easily from the palms of your hands. Practice by kneeling on the floor and placing a thick cushion in front of you. Lean forward and rest your palms on it. Breathe in. As you breathe out, move your body weight over your hands and apply pressure. As you do this, I suggest you imagine breathing chi into the other person.

IMPROVED CIRCULATION

Pummeling or pounding the surface of the body encourages better circulation and activates chi. Keep your wrists limp, so that the motion stems from your elbows. Your hands should flop up and down on relaxed wrists. The lightest technique involves using your fingertips; the sides of your hands, palms, loose fists, and two hands clasped together become progressively stronger. Certain parts of the body (such as the skull) need to be treated delicately while others (such the buttocks) can be pounded vigorously.

RELAXING TIGHT, KNOTTED MUSCLES

When muscles have been in motion for an extended period of time, they start to produce lactic acid. If this by-product accumulates and remains in the muscle fibers, it prevents them from sliding across each other and regaining their full length. As a result, muscles stay contracted, which can lead to tightness, stiffness, and eventual loss of mobility.

To get rid of lactic acid build-up and improve circulation, softly squeeze body tissues using kneading movements . When giving a shiatsu, find out how firmly your partner likes to be massaged. You can either grab the skin between your thumb and fingers or gently squeeze it between your fingers and palm. Give your kneading a certain rhythm to stimulate a regular flow of chi energy into the muscle tissue.

Regular stretching frees up the chi trapped in knotted muscles and shiatsu has the power to release stagnant chi and the pent-up emotions that go with it. Stretch your partner slowly and work on discovering the boundaries of his/her comfort zone.

MANIPULATING JOINTS

The joints in the body become stiff and lose mobility through daily wear and tear. Flexing the joints is part and parcel of any dynamic shiatsu treatment. Experiment on yourself first to understand which joints move in which direction, then manipulate those same joints in a similar way on a friend or partner. Avoid exerting undue pressure or force at any time.

YOUR INSTRUMENTS

Learn to apply pressure and project chi using various parts of the body.

1 **Hands**
The easiest to start with. They provide even pressure over large areas.

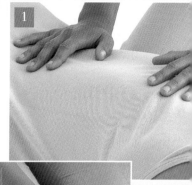

2 **Thumbs**
Ideal for applying detailed and localized pressure to specific acupressure points.

3 **Elbows**
Useful for applying strong pressure over small areas in targeted parts of the body such as the shoulders, buttocks, or upper legs.

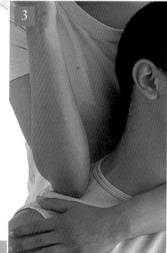

4 **Knees**
Effective for distributing strong pressure over large body areas.

5 **Feet**
Ideally suited to giving massage as they can cover a wide location, provide considerable pressure, and are soft and flexible. The least tiring to use.

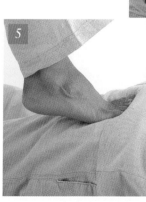

GIVING A SHIATSU

Ask your partner to sit on a chair or kneel on the floor. Rest your hands on his/her shoulders and follow his/her breathing. Gently and rhythmically squeeze his/her shoulders, kneading the muscles with both hands. Next, place your fingers, thumbs, elbows, or both hands (see page 39) over the muscle that runs across the top of his/her shoulders. Lean forward, pressing into the muscle as you breathe out, working from the neck to the shoulders.

With a loose fist and relaxed wrists, pound your partner's shoulders 1. Place your hands on his/her shoulders to check whether his/her breathing has changed.

Ask your partner to lie face down. Use layers of towels to make this position more comfortable. If your partner has a stiff neck, put a cushion under his/her chest. Feel his/her breathing.

Stand or kneel astride your partner. Place your palms on his/her upper back 2. Breathe in. On the out-breath, lean your body weight on your hands. Work down his/her back continuing to press on each exhalation. Repeat, but this time, apply pressure through your thumbs either side of your partner's spine as you work your way down toward his/her buttocks.

Next, firmly and rhythmically press the ball of your foot into your partner's buttock 3. Rock his/her body from side to side to loosen up the back joints effectively.

Kneel beside your partner's upper leg, place your hand on his/her lower back and lift his/her foot while slowly pressing his/her thigh with your knee 4. Massage from the top of the leg toward the kneecap.

Put his/her foot back on the ground and kneel next to your partner's lower leg. Run your thumb down the center of his/her calf muscle starting at the back of the knee 5. There is a powerful acupressure point one-third of the way down. Repeat with the other leg. Move down until you reach your partner's feet. Make sure that the

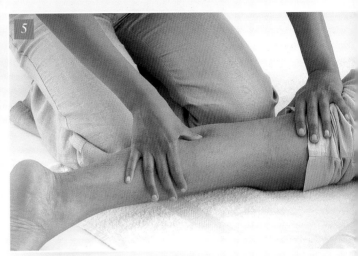

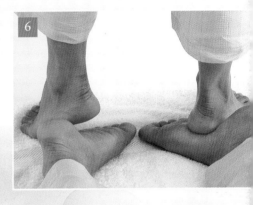

toes are pointing inward and the heels facing outward. Standing on your toes, massage the soles of his/her feet with your heels 6.

Keeping a hold of the ankles, proceed to lift his/her knees to stretch the front part of his/her thighs and abdomen 7.

Place your partner's knees back down on the floor. Holding the balls of his/her feet, gently push the feet down toward the ground to get a full stretch along the backs of the ankles 8. Push your partner's feet up

toward his/her buttocks stretching the front of his/her legs 9. Finish by placing your hands on your partner's back. Reconnect with his/her breathing pattern.

KINESIOLOGY

MUSCLE TESTING
Ask your partner to relax and contemplate your question as he/she slowly breathes deeply in and out. Place your palms over his/her wrists as he/she moves both arms out to the sides and you provide resistance.

I have found that the human body possesses an inherent capacity to heal itself. Kinesiology is a feedback tool that operates according to this principle. Chi energy theory tells us that objects or feelings not in harmony with your chi energy field could result in slight and temporary muscle weakness during muscle-testing. Likewise, thinking about something upsetting or troubling could also change your chi, making it harder for you to exert maximum force.

MANUAL MUSCLE TESTING

The kinesiologist applies firm resistance during muscle testing by holding down the straight arms of the patient, then asking him/her to try to move them. An assessment is made based on the muscular force exerted by the recipient. Such sensitivity is useful in the hands of an expert when probing and seeking to treat the underlying causes of disease or discomfort. This idea can also be applied to your body's symmetry. In a relaxed state, your body should be evenly balanced. Sudden, dramatic changes to energy flow can result in physical disturbances across the body.

In order to find answers through muscle-testing, the recipient's mind will need to be relaxed and open-minded. Don't try to pre-empt the answers. If you're working on a friend, carry out some preliminary sample-testing on his/her arm under ideal conditions as a point of reference.

I suggest you ask questions that solicit either "yes" or "no" responses. Start with general lines of enquiry, then home in on details once the session is in full swing. If someone has a skin rash, for example, and you want to ascertain whether he/she has some deeper knowledge of its cause, you might ask something like "Does food make your rash worse?" before re-testing your friend's arm. If this question produces a weak response, you can begin to enquire about different aspects of food, starting with the major food groups such as dairy, wheat, sugar, fruits, and nuts; then, with a weak response for any of these groups, you can go on to examine the exact types of foods within that category for more information.

If you did not get a weak response to food at all, you can broach other areas. With a dermatological flare-up, for example, other potential causes could include clothing, stress, and allergies to cosmetics or soaps. Once you have located a possible cause for your friend's problem, he/she can eliminate the suspected culprit and see if there is a positive result or a change.

In my experience, the accuracy of muscle testing depends on asking the right questions. With practice, you will be able to conduct the whole process in such a way that others find reassuring and calming.

USING THE WRISTS

1 Ask your partner to lie face down on the floor. Stand astride his/her legs and pick up both wrists. Place them over the center of the body, in line with the spine, and evenly pull each wrist toward the feet.

2 If your partner is relaxed, the ends, knuckles, and joints of the thumbs should line up. If not, massage the shoulder and back. Try again. Ask your question. After your partner has considered it, re-check his/her hands.

3 Put your partner's hands back down on the floor each time you ask a question. Restore them to an even position by massaging your partner's upper back and shoulders while he/she thinks pleasant thoughts before asking the next question.

USING A PENDULUM TO LOCATE THE CHAKRAS

CHAKRAS

Chakras are centers of intense, swirling chi activity at specific points along your body through which your spiritual and emotional energies flow. Learning to locate the chakras on a partner (who is lying down) by using a pendulum, which is influenced by chi energy, will be useful for subsequent exercises. Tie one yard (one meter) of cotton thread around a metal ring. Suspend it over those parts of your partner that you want to assess. Hold the end of the cord so the ring is free to move. Watch for signs that it is beginning to swing. When you have found a chakra, the ring will begin to circle on the end of its cord. The direction in which it circles reflects the way this energy spirals. If nothing happens, slowly move the ring away and try again.

LOCATIONS AND PROPERTIES

THE CROWN CHAKRA (SAHASRARA)
To find this chakra, ask your partner to sit on a chair or kneel on the floor. Inspect his/her head at the crown to find a wavy spiral in the hair. Suspend the ring over this area and find the spot where it begins to swing or circle. The Crown Chakra is a highly influential entry point, where chi enters the body with greatest ease and flows into the main channel that links all the seven chakras. The Crown Chakra points to the sky through the head to draw in chi from around the planet, while balancing the internal and external energies of the individual. This energy gives you the capacity to be intuitive and spiritually connected.

THE MIDBRAIN CHAKRA (AJNA)
Situated between your eyebrows, the Midbrain Chakra can be located by holding the pendulum over the center of your partner's forehead (who is lying down). This type of chi relates to the ability to think, the intellect, and powers of reason. Known as "the third eye," this chakra corresponds with the part of the brain used for planning. When the Midbrain Chakra is particularly active, you may experience interesting flashes and fascinating insights.

THE THROAT CHAKRA (VISHUDDHI)

In males, this chakra is located at the front of the neck at the height of the Adam's apple. In females, it is found in the middle of the throat. To activate it, hold the ring over your partner's neck. The Throat Chakra is associated with creativity and communication: this is where the chi of your heart and mind meet to form your out-breath and words. This chakra acts as a balancing-point and should be activated to restore lost emotional and mental stability. Talking, singing, and chanting are also helpful since energy is experienced through sound vibrations in the Throat Chakra.

THE HEART CHAKRA (ANHATA)

Located between the nipples when lying down, find the Heart Chakra by pressing the slight indentation there on your partner before positioning the pendulum over this area. It contains the chi of your emotions and is the center of feelings of love, harmony, and peace. If you keep the chi here moving freely, you will be able to overcome emotional upsets and traumas more quickly.

THE STOMACH CHAKRA (NABHI)

Located in the solar plexus, find the Stomach Chakra by suspending the pendulum over the area between your partner's chest and navel until it starts to swing. If the chi of the Stomach Chakra is overly active, people become work-obsessed; if there is too little energy here, listlessness and lethargy follow. This type of chi is the driving force of life.

THE ABDOMEN CHAKRA (MOOLADHARA)

Also called the *hara*, the Abdomen Chakra is found two finger-widths below the navel so hold the pendulum just above it. This area should be slightly raised when your partner is lying on his/her back for maximum energy intake. The *hara* is considered to be the source of inner chi and nourishes the other chakras giving you power, physical endurance, and mental stamina. In ancient Japan, people would wear a cotton band, called a *hara maki*, to keep this region warm and protected.

THE SEX CHAKRA (SWADISTHAN)

Located between the anus and the genital organs in males and females, this chakra is also known as the Base Chakra, and contains the chi primarily focused on sex, reproductive capacity, and physical pleasure. Find it by suspending the pendulum ring over your partner's pubic bone.

TUNING IN TO SOMEONE ELSE'S THOUGHTS AND EMOTIONS

MEDITATION /
VISUALIZATION

In my view, developing your sensitivity to chi and, by implication, that of other people's, will help you tune in to another's thoughts and emotions. This can open up a whole new world, where you become more perceptive and intuitive about the people around you. As you develop these skills, it becomes easier to understand others and relate more deeply to their emotional state. Ultimately, it is rather like being able to access the contents of someone else's heart and mind.

THOUGHTS

Ask your partner to sit down or kneel. Your hands should be able to comfortably reach his/her head. Start with the chi-generating exercise on pages 32-33.

Ask your partner to concentrate on his/her breathing. Bring your hands close to and away from his/her head to register areas that are hot or have a strong magnetic pull. Make a sketch of the head and write notes. If your partner is bald or has very short hair, mark the hotter areas with "Post-it" notes. For longer hair, indicate the location of these areas by tying colored thread.

Next your partner should concentrate on a future event, prospect, or wish. Make sure that he/she does not slip into thinking about the past. Recommend rolling up the eyes as if looking at the inside of the forehead. Feel your partner's head, especially the forehead. Note down any areas that feel noticeably warmer.

Ask your partner to close his/her eyes and recall a past event in great detail. Move your hands over your partner's head concentrating on the back. Make a note of hot spots or places with a strong magnetic pull.

Rest for a few minutes. Get your partner to clear his/her mind before returning to a previous thought. Feel the chi around his/her head. Work out if your partner is imagining something new or retracing a past event.

EMOTIONS

This exercise teaches you how to recognize different emotions and link them to the flow of chi within particular parts of the navel. During this technique, your partner must be willing to relive an event that conjures up strong emotions.

The chi flowing below the navel relates to feelings of fear and anxiety. The chi that flows to your right of the navel is connected with frustration and anger. Directly above the belly button, the dominant emotional state is hysteria; at the center, envy and jealousy rule; to your left of the navel, depression is the key emotion.

Ask your partner to lie down on his/her back and to focus on his/her breathing until it becomes level and regular. Gently probe your partner's abdomen with your fingertips to feel the localized chi in this area. Look out for those places that feel soft or relaxed and make a mental note of where they are located. Identify a strong pulse around the midriff and record how it feels.

Ask your partner to recall an emotionally charged event while you move your hand over his/her abdomen in search of new hot spots or areas with a strong magnetic pull. Gently probe the abdomen once again to detect changes. Search for areas that have hardened or tensed up. Find the pulse again. Make a note of any areas that feel warmer.

Compare whether the changes that you noticed relate to these specific areas and their relevant emotions. Check your notes against what your partner felt.

After a few minutes' rest, request your partner either think of something calming or laden with emotion. See if you can assess what he/she is thinking from how his/her abdomen feels.

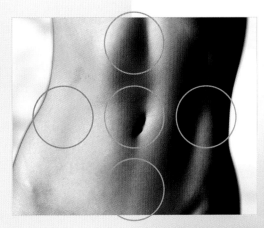

○ **HEART CHI**
Hysteria

○ **LUNGS CHI**
Depression

○ **SPLEEN CHI**
Envy, Jealousy

○ **LIVER CHI**
Anger, Frustration

○ **KIDNEY CHI**
Fear, Anxiety

Chi ENERGY
WORKBOOK

Chi ENERGY
AND THE MIND

If you are able to direct and exercise control over your mental chi, you can then channel positive thoughts to kickstart your day, expand or cleanse your mind through meditation techniques, and manipulate acupressure points to mobilize trapped chi. The kinds of foods that you eat and teas that you drink are also important in boosting mental chi. Implement specific feng shui recommendations to reorganize your living space into an empowering area where you can sleep peacefully and think clearly.

USING YOUR MIND TO CHANGE YOUR CHI

BREATHING

You can influence and change the energy around you by triggering thoughts that then stimulate physiological reactions. These responses require and give off energy in the form of chi. Your brain not only has the capacity to "color" your inner chi, but also can direct it into different parts of your body. I will show you different techniques to focus your mind and develop concentration skills. Because the brain has such incredible powers to focus chi, you can use it to control and gradually shift the direction of the energy flowing inside you. Learn to move chi down, up, outward, or inward, depending on your needs. This practice is enhanced when mental thought is combined with the correct breathing techniques. In our everyday life, most of us use only about 10 percent of our total mental capacity; mobilizing chi through the power of your mind can help you make more of this amazing tool. Perform the chi-moving exercises below in a quiet and peaceful place.

MENTAL MANIPULATION OF CHI

In the initial stages of learning to exercise control over your mental chi, it is helpful to associate this force with an object or an activity that naturally speaks to you. You will usually find the strongest influences to be visual, auditory, or touch sensations. For example, your preferred method of relaxation might be to watch a film, observe a sunset, or visit an art gallery. As these experiences are all highly visual, their associated imagery will prove effective when you try to re-live that same state of relaxation, perhaps during a visualization or meditation exercise. If you discover that the best way to unwind is by talking to a friend, listening to relaxing music, or playing an instrument, you will be most susceptible to sound and its vibrations. If you respond naturally to the sensation of touch, having a massage, being in a sauna, or doing some form of physical exercise will be most conducive to mentally channeling your chi.

Once you have identified which "setting" works best for you, use it as a powerful prompt for mentally accessing and actively manipulating chi. If you discover that you react best to visual stimulation, for example, try to imagine your chi as a color or strong light. Picture taking this hue into your body on the in-breath and different parts of your body absorbing it on the out-breath.

If sounds are your strongest stimuli, define your chi in auditory terms. Imagine you are breathing in a sound that floods into your body and can be moved to where more energy is required. Similarly, if you respond to touch, visualize breathing in warmth or heat that gradually spreads through your body. Shift this sensation to other parts of your body as you breathe out.

When you feel confident using these sensory channels, you can combine them in interesting ways: breathe in a cool, blue color as the sound of waves crash on the shore, for instance. Find and utilize objects or situations that act as powerful triggers and mentally earmark those visual images, sounds, and touch sensations that have the greatest significance for you.

GETTING RID OF A HEADACHE

Help someone cure a raging headache by simply asking him or her the following questions:

Where is the headache?

Is the pain you suffer near the surface or deep inside your head?

If the pain you feel had a color, what would it be?

If the pain you have made a sound, what would it be?

Can you describe the shape of the pain?

On a score from 1-10, how intense is the pain?

Encourage the other person to answer these questions in full and repeat this sequence of questions several times until the discomfort disappears or subsides. If you're dealing with a stubborn headache, such as a migraine, ask your friend to alter the color of the pain to a gentle pastel shade, modify its sound to a more soothing tone, and alter its contour to a softer shape. To increase relaxation, investigate what makes the sufferer feel happy—perhaps lying on a beach, swimming in the sea, listening to an inspiring piece of music, walking through a summer garden, or watching a breathtaking sunset. Encourage him/her to actually "feel" being there. When you have a severe headache, get someone else to guide you through this exercise.

MOVING CHI DOWN

Useful for feeling down-to-earth, practical, and grounded. Ideal for when your head is preoccupied with thoughts and you cannot find peace of mind.

1 Sit down in a chair. Inhale gently through your nostrils. Imagine your breath going up into your head. Feel it becoming colder as it flows across the roof of your mouth. Mix the air with the chi and your thoughts so that you can expel them as you breathe out.

2 As you breathe out, release all the air from your chest, then your abdomen, trying to retain this last bit of air until the very end. Repeat until comfortable. On the out-breath, as you release air from your upper chest and move it down to your lower abdomen, breathe chi down your legs into your feet.

3 Imagine breathing chi through your feet. Feel them getting a little warmer as you try to push increasingly deeper into the ground. Relax and concentrate on your feet. Feel your body drawing up fresh energy from the earth and moving it toward your head. Repeat several times a day.

MOVING CHI UP

Perfect when you are looking for new ideas and need to get more energy into your head. Encourages you to feel more positive, active, and outgoing.

1 Stand with your feet shoulder-width apart. Lean forward with your weight over the balls of your feet. Breathe into your abdomen, then your chest. Exhale, emptying your abdomen fully before releasing the final bout of air from your upper chest. Imagine chi shifting from your abdomen into your head.

2 Once comfortable with the technique involved in step 1, let your arms hang down by your sides, palms facing front. On the out-breath, slowly raise your hands, lifting them up close to the front of the body until they reach your upper chest. Come up on tiptoes as you approach the end of the exhalation.

3 Feel a light mental buzz as energy enters your head. Relax and focus your mind on drawing chi into your head through the Crown Chakra. Allow the energy flowing into your head to slowly drift down through your body. This motion will encourage more chi intake via the Crown Chakra.

EXPANDING CHI OUTWARD

Good for making a great first impression, expressing yourself, and releasing negative emotions. Accompany with skin scrubbing and deep, chest-pounding breathing exercises on the exhale. Expanding this energy too widely could result in loss of inner strength.

Crouch down with your feet shoulder-width apart. Fold your arms across your chest. Inhale and imagine that you are taking in a wealth of chi. Feel this energy rushing into your body, energizing you, and filling up your lungs.

As you exhale, stand up and thrust your arms out into a star shape. Imagine releasing chi through the tips of your fingers and toes. Feel this energy expanding in a wide circle. Make an "ahh" sound to radiate it out further.

DRAWING CHI INWARD

Useful for developing inner strength by tapping into your deepest chi core. Helpful when you are feeling tired, cold, or fragile. Filling up this source of energy will allow you to find solutions to deep-seated problems. If too much chi is held in, however, you risk diminishing your chi connection with the outside world and this can result in a build-up of negative emotions.

Kneel or sit down. Inhale through your nostrils. Draw chi into your abdomen, then up into your chest. Clench your anus as you tighten your abdominal muscles, keeping your mouth and nasal passages closed. Feel heat spreading into your abdomen. Imagine inwardly compressing chi. Exhale slowly. Repeat and rest.

THE FIRST THOUGHT OF THE DAY

MEDITATION /
VISUALIZATION

Your mind usually feels rested and relatively free of thought when you first wake up in the morning. This mental space is created during the night as you release accumulated emotion through the complex process of dreaming. This is why the moment when you first open your eyes is the ideal time to have the one important thought that starts your day. To help this, begin your day with a meditation practice to help you generate and maintain empowering chi energy close to you—the fuel keeping you on track during the course of the day. Because you will inevitably come into contact with different types of energy, it is imperative to set off with a head full of positive energy.

If you practice this simple sequence on a regular basis, it will become easier to cultivate the emotional levels that you desire. Focus on small things to begin with in order to build your confidence, see how this works for you, and then move on to bigger, more ambitious targets. Later, when you lie in bed that night, think back to your day. Did you come close to experiencing the feelings that you'd dreamt about once you'd chosen the type of emotional chi you wanted to flow through every cell of your body?

CHANNELING YOUR THOUGHTS

As soon as you wake up, get out of bed and give your body a long and thorough stretch. If your limbs feel tired or cramped, use meridian stretches (see page 130) to bring them back to life. If you struggle to get up, try doing lying-down stretches in bed to make this transition a little easier.

Once you have finished stretching, sit up or kneel with the front of your body facing the rising sun in the East. Rest your hands on your legs with your palms facing up to encourage your chi to ascend. This position lets you directly absorb more of the sun's chi energy and helps you to feel increasingly ready and willing to start the day. Sit up with your back straight. Adjust your head by pulling your jaw back slightly and raising the back of your head so your Crown Chakra is pointing upward. Imagine this chakra is being suspended by a thread and that your neck and spine are hanging from it.

Empty your mind by concentrating on your breathing. Feel every drop of air entering and leaving your body. Breathe into your abdomen first, then your chest. As you exhale, relax your chest followed by your stomach. Breathe freely and easily. Once in tune with your breathing and with a clear mind, start to focus on how you would like to feel when the day comes to a close.

Concentrate on one feeling at a time. For example, you might choose to feel content, satisfied, calm, loved, secure, independent, enthusiastic, or in harmony with other people.

FOCUSING YOUR INTENT

When you have identified how you want to feel, "become" that feeling— imagine being enveloped by it before you go to bed. Analyze what you need to do to end up feeling this way. Consider any hurdles you may have to face during the day. Focus on the qualities you want to have and let thoughts float through your mind as you search for inspiration. Relax and, once your ideas are in place, write them down. Meditate on whatever strengths will help you to achieve this. You may need to be more patient, confrontational, honest, focused, considerate, disciplined, responsible, or easygoing. Become familiar with this feeling—how it works, what its boundaries are—and repeatedly revisit it during the day to energize yourself.

THE POWER OF THE MORNING STRETCH
As soon as you wake up, get out of bed and enliven your body with a long, natural, feelgood stretch. During sleep, muscles may bunch up in one area and there are physiological and psychological benefits from taking a few minutes out of your day to stretch and relax.

FOOD FOR CLARITY OF THOUGHT

FOOD

SEAWEED WONDER
Include cleansing "sea vegetables" in your diet like edible wakame which is similar to kombu in appearance, but much softer in texture.

Living in today's hectic and polluted world means that we all come to absorb toxins from our environment. One way to fight this intrusion on our health is to equip our diet with many different varieties of seaweed or "sea vegetables." Choose from Japanese kombu, wakame, nori, or dulse (the Irish equivalent), capable of isolating toxins in the blood to aid their disposal as waste products. The following pages outline a healthy diet to detoxify your body.

What we eat influences how and what we feel. Eating the right kind of food in terms of your chi energy can make an incredible difference to your long-term wellbeing and overall emotional state.

When you chew, the muscles that stretch from your jawline to above your temples massage the sides of your head and help to move chi around your brain. Aim to masticate every mouthful at least 30 times, prolonging the time that you keep the chi of the food in your mouth before swallowing. Mix food in well with the saliva of your mouth, so that enzymes can initiate a chemical process that enables better digestion and absorption.

I believe that whatever you eat will ultimately reach and influence the make-up of your brain through digestive assimilation. Your concentration, mental focus, memory, and emotional balance are all directly linked to the quality of your diet. To my mind, not only will nutrients influence your moods and brain-power, but so, too, will the chi of the foods that you eat. Thinking about food positively and eating a well-balanced diet high in minerals with plenty of living chi, refreshes the mind and promotes renewed mental powers. This process of mental uncluttering leads to increased clarity of thought as all of the brain cells are being flooded with vibrant energy.

Your meals are primarily absorbed through the small intestine, where they are processed, transferred to the liver, and fed into your bloodstream. Once in your circulatory system, they will help define your blood chemistry and flood to your brain cells. Minerals, sugars, and fats (see box) can strongly affect your mental state.

POSITIVE AND NEGATIVE NUTRIENTS

Mineral-rich types of ingredients are considered healthy brain food. Refined sugars and saturated fats, however, are non-productive types of nutrients. The refined sugars accelerate and activate your inner chi to such an extent that you come to feel hyperactive and manic, while saturated fats can adversely influence the structure of your brain and the way it functions, risking a general slowing down.

MINERALS

Vital for the growth and repair of cells and the regulation of body processes, minerals are essential to a good memory and concentration. Ensure that you eat plenty of fish, seeds, vegetables, and seaweed in order to maintain mineral levels, particularly if you eat lots of sugary foods.

SUGARS

Refined sugars are absorbed into your bloodstream via the tongue and stomach lining. They quickly raise blood sugar levels and cause a rush of sugar to your brain. In a dramatic reaction aimed at lowering blood sugar levels, your body can trigger so much insulin, released through the pancreas, that the blood sugar concentration ends up being too low. Feelings of depression, insecurity, and lethargy are caused by low sugar and chi levels. A regular intake of processed sugars increases the risk of repetitive disturbance to your inner chi making it harder for you to contain the energy necessary to develop inner balance.

SATURATED FATS

As they flow through the fine capillaries of the brain, saturated fats thicken the blood to produce an overall clogging effect. These types of fats slow down (and even stop) the flow of chi to parts of the brain. This results in a sluggish head, a reluctance to embrace change or new prospects, and a lack of flexibility.

A VARIED DIET

In choosing foods to provide you with the kind of chi that you need, consider how they have been grown. For example, parsley, leeks, and spring onions grow up through the soil and so will contain a strong, upward current of chi. If you want to feel uplifted, include more of these types of vegetables in your diet. The opposite would be true of root vegetables, which grow down into the earth. I recommend this variety of chi for feeling grounded and stable. Certain vegetables, like squash, grow along the ground; this balanced method of growth encourages chi to be more centrally contained, making it easier to feel content and satisfied.

Think about food also in terms of where it is in its life cycle. Seeds, grains, and beans are all very "young" foods, ready to be sown and grown into a new plant. They contain a fresh, youthful energy compared to vegetables, fish, or meat, which are fully mature foods in terms of their chi content. At the other end of the food energy spectrum, fermented foods (like pickles, wine, and miso) have been broken down, having completed their life cycle. This type of chi encourages wisdom and good judgment. Interestingly, these foods can also represent the beginning of a new phase as they contain primal bacteria. By eating these foods, you can stimulate the most primitive chi in your body to increase sexual vigor and the powers of survival.

You will obtain far more chi through whole "living" foods like brown rice, whole oats, barley, vegetables, fruits, nuts, seeds, and beans. When buying fresh fish and meat, consider the character and behavior of the animals involved as this will reflect the type of energy that you are absorbing. The more aggressive the creature, the more of that particular chi you will be taking in.

When advising people about their health, nutritional habits, and lifestyle, I have found the best overall diet for mental and emotional wellbeing to be one that is high in complex carbohydrates. These long chains of sugar molecules break down slowly in the body and help to keep blood sugar levels stable. As a result, emotions are more constant and this equilibrium helps to take the edge off sharp mood swings.

Another key to a long-term healthy diet is variety. If you include a wide range of ingredients and cook them in versatile ways, the risk of actual nutritional deficiency becomes negligible. Most dietary problems occur when you eat too much of one thing (even if it happens to be healthy) or if the range is too limited, so benefit from eating a large variety of chi-rich foods.

Your body has a natural capacity to make you crave the foods it needs, but can only do this if exposed to a wide selection. It can then make associations between the flavors, nutrients, and energy contained in those foods. These biological signals should not be confused with the emotional cravings caused by a desire to conjure up feelings associated with certain foods, particularly high-sugar, fatty comfort foods like chocolates and ice cream.

I suggest that you eat organic foods as often as possible to reduce your exposure to pesticides, colorants, and other additives. This is especially pertinent with dairy products, meat and fish, as cattle and fish are often fed steroids, growth hormones, antibiotics, and dyes, all of which end up inside you. There is a general rule to follow when it comes to processed foods—the more natural the product, the shorter its ingredients list will be.

FRUITY HEIGHTS
Some fruits, like apples, peaches, and bananas, grow on branches suspended high up in the air. The chi from these foods helps to heighten your spiritual connection with the cosmos, although an excess of it will result in a loss of pragmatism and connection with the earth.

CHI FOODS

FOOD TYPE	WHAT THEY DO	EXAMPLES
Stimulating	Help you to become uplifted and inspired. They encourage mental activity that stimulates new and creative ideas.	Leeks, scallions, celery, leafy green vegetables, parsley, kale, spring greens, Chinese cabbage, watercress, chives, bok choy.
Grounding	Allow you to feel stable and secure. They increase your inner strength and greatly enhance your powers of concentration.	Carrots, parsnips, burdock, daikon.
Balancing	Make you feel contented, satisfied, and centered, as they are good at containing inner chi.	Squash, potatoes, rutabaga, cabbage, cauliflower, broccoli, melon.
Far-reaching	Grow away from the ground and help to elevate you spiritually.	Apples, pears, oranges, tomatoes, grapes, apricots.
Young chi-containing	Preserve physical and mental elasticity and revitalize you.	Brown rice, oats, barley, sesame seeds, pumpkin seeds, sunflower seeds, lentils, Adzuki beans, chickpeas.
Mature chi-containing	Stabilize the emotions to make you feel secure and content.	Fish, meat, vegetables, fruits, seaweed, potatoes.
Chi flow-enhancing	Help you to "go with the flow" and help you feel more relaxed.	Squid, shrimp, mussels, clams, flounder.
Assertive	Give you the courage and determination to fight for what you want.	Wild salmon, eel, mackerel, tuna, shark.
Wisdom / primal	Strengthen your ability to act wisely and your deepest primal instincts for sex and survival.	Miso, pickles, yogurt, wine, beer, shoyu.

MENUS CONDUCIVE TO GOOD CHI

The ultimate "brain food" diet is one high in fish, seafood, grains, vegetables, seaweed, fruit, nuts, and seeds. Below are several of my menu and recipe suggestions for you to try out. Persevere with this eating plan for at least 10 days to get an accurate idea of how it affects your body and mind. During this time, avoid anything with added sugar, so read all ingredient labels carefully.

BREAKFAST

- Peppermint, ginger, or lemon tea. (These invigorating teas will perk and wake you up, and get you off to a vibrant start.)

- Porridge made from whole oats and flavored with roasted sunflower seeds and raisins. (This provides you with slow burning fuel for the rest of the day.)

- Creamy polenta with maple syrup and roasted sesame seeds. (Although processed and not quite so high in "living" chi, this dish is still smooth, comforting, and easily absorbed. Ideal if you want a more gentle start to the day.)

- Steamed bread with tahini paste and wild or organic smoked salmon with a dash of lemon juice and chive garnish. (This dish will give you the assertiveness to go out and make things happen. Steaming the bread makes it more digestible and gentler on the stomach. The lemon gives you that little bit of extra sharpness and the chives a get-up-and-go energy.)

LUNCH

- Sushi or maguro maki (tuna rolls) and salad. (When combined with a side salad, this cold Japanese dish offers a good mix of seaweed, fish, rice, and wasabi—which has a pungent taste similar to horseradish—and is a complete meal full of the nutrients you need for a productive afternoon.)

- Hummus sandwich with pickles and lemon, mixed with little spicy peppers as an optional extra. (This serving suggestion is a good staple for emotional stability and helpful during times of stress.)

- Corn on the cob with blanched carrots, broccoli, and greens seasoned with natural vinegar. (This lunch option is high in "living" chi with a good mix of upward-, centered-, and downward-moving energies. It is light and fresh and the vinegar sharpens the mind.)

- Drink water.

MID-MORNING SNACK

- Roasted nuts with fruit juice, water, or green tea. (Nuts are full of minerals, proteins, and oils. Fruit juice is mentally stimulating, good-quality water adds an element of purity, and green tea has a cleansing and calming influence.)

MID-AFTERNOON SNACK

- Roasted seeds, raisins, or a piece of fruit with fruit tea or water. (Nuts and raisins are a rich source of minerals and proteins. Fruit contains vitamins and minerals. Water, fruit juice, and tea are all good internal cleansers.)

DINNER

- Miso soup with wakame seaweed, leafy greens, and a dash of ginger juice, or thick lentil and root vegetable soup garnished with parsley and a slice of lemon. (This type of soup is rich in minerals and the vegetables are full of the upward-moving chi that stimulates the mind. Ginger further activates this type of chi, while the combination of lentils and root vegetables make this a mentally strengthening dish. Lemon and parsley add a bit of extra spark.)

- Fried brown rice with garlic, ginger, and parsley, or noodles in broth with vegetables, or fried soba noodles and vegetables. Brown rice provides long-term stable chi, frying ginger and garlic will stimulate the mind, and adding finely chopped up parsley will help to drive chi up into your head. Noodles in broth with vegetables quickly raise the body's temperature and are ideal for releasing surplus mental chi outward. Frying the noodles and vegetables adds additional fiery energy. Eat this dish immediately for an optimum absorption that will send an instant burst of energy to your mind.

- Stewed, blanched, and pressed vegetables. (Try to accompany most of your meals with a side order of vegetables. Stewing is the best method of preparation if you want to be able to concentrate on one thing for an extended period of time; blanching is recommended if you want to get fresh ideas; pressing is preferable for an open mind receptive to new ideas.)

- Fish. (Eat different kinds of fish 2-3 times a week. This could include adding fish to miso soup, prawns to vegetable stew, or dried fish flakes to the noodle broth.)

- Raw or cooked fruit. (If you boil or steam fruit, more chi will be retained in the center of your body, making it easier for you to find emotional stability. Raw fruit helps expand your mind.)

- Camomile tea. (This drink helps calm your mind and makes you sleep well.)

Ginger, a root vegetable, is available in fresh, dried, and ground form and imparts a distinctive taste.

CHI-BOOSTING RECIPES

> **ALL RECIPES SERVE 4 PEOPLE**

POLENTA WITH SYRUP

- 1 cup organic polenta
- 4 tbsp sesame seeds
- maple syrup (to taste)

Place the polenta in 4 cups of cold water in a pan. Bring to a boil, reduce the flame, and put a flame deflector under the pan. Uncover. Simmer for 10-15 minutes and stir. Add the seeds. Switch off and divide into 4 serving bowls. Add syrup to taste.

WHOLE OAT PORRIDGE WITH RAISINS AND SUNFLOWER SEEDS

- 1 cup whole oats
- ¼ cup raisins
- 4 tbsp toasted sunflower seeds
- 1 tbsp toasted sesame seeds

Bring the oats to a boil in a covered pan. Reduce the flame, uncover, and simmer for 1 hour. Add the raisins. Cook for another 5 minutes, stirring occasionally as raisins tend to stick. Switch off and leave to stand overnight. Heat up carefully in the morning. Divide into 4 serving bowls. Serve with the seeds.

MISO SOUP

- 1 3-inch wakame seaweed strip
- 1 tbsp miso paste (barley miso is best)
- 1 handful of watercress and 2 Chinese cabbage leaves, finely chopped
- 2 sheets of nori seaweed, cut into fine strips
- ½ tsp grated ginger
- 8 1-inch cubes of cod (optional)

Pre-soak the wakame strip in a bowl for 2 minutes. Bring 4 cups of water to a boil in a pan and reduce the flame to simmer. Add the wakame strip. Turn off the heat. Put the miso paste in a cup and dilute it with 2 tablespoons of cold water. Heat up the wakame again. Add in the miso mixture and simmer gently for 3 minutes. Add the watercress and Chinese cabbage leaves and turn off the heat. Serve with fine-cut strips of nori. Add a pinch of grated ginger. If you want to include fish in the recipe, add cubes of cod with the wakame.

Shiitake mushrooms can be bought in fresh or dried form.

LENTIL SOUP

- 1 cup green lentils
- 2 celery stalks, diced
- 1 medium carrot, diced
- 2 bay leaves
- 1 tsp sea salt
- 2 tbsp sunflower oil
- ½ tsp turmeric
- ½ tsp cumin
- 5 fresh shiitake mushrooms, diced
- 3 small scallions, finely diced
- 4 lemon slices (to garnish)

Wash the lentils in 3 cups of warm water in a pan. Soak overnight. The following day, bring them to a boil in the same water. Cook for 10 minutes. Switch off the heat. In a cast-iron or enameled pan, place the celery, carrot, and lentils. Add the bay leaves. Pour in 1 quart of water. Cover. Bring to a boil. Reduce the flame to medium and cook for 15-20 minutes. Halfway through, add the salt. Heat the oil, turmeric, and cumin in a pan. Fry for 1-2 minutes. Add the mushrooms and scallions and sauté for 1 minute. Pour the mixture into the soup. Simmer for 2 minutes. Serve with a slice of lemon.

SOBA SPICE

- 1 packet of cooked soba noodles
- 1 tbsp sesame oil (or toasted sesame oil in winter)
- 1 small onion, sliced
- 1 large carrot, cut into matchsticks
- 2 celery stalks
- 4 Chinese cabbage leaves, sliced
- 4 tbsp shoyu
- 2 tbsp grated ginger

After cooking the noodles, drain and rinse them thoroughly. Heat the oil in a large wok or frying pan. Add the onion and stir-fry for 1 minute, then the carrot and celery. Quickly stir-fry for 2 minutes. Add the noodles and mix in well with the vegetables. Add the cabbage leaves. Season with shoyu. Remove from the heat. Squeeze ginger over the mixture.

NOODLES

- 1 packet of cooked udon or soba noodles
- 3 1-inch kombu pieces
- 4 small shiitake mushrooms
- ¼ tsp sea salt
- 1 cup bonito flakes (optional)
- 1 small onion, sliced in half-moons
- 1 small carrot, cut into matchsticks
- ¼ cup shoyu
- 1 tbsp mirin (or sake)
- 1 small scallion, finely cut diagonally
- 2 sheets of nori seaweed, finely cut
- shichimi (to taste)

After cooking the noodles, drain and rinse them thoroughly and set them aside. To make the broth, place the kombu, shiitake, and salt in 4 cups of water in a pan. Bring to a boil on a medium flame. Place the flakes in a sieve and cover with water. Simmer for 5 minutes. Remove the kombu and the shiitake. Discard the stems, slice, and put the mushrooms back in the pan. Add the onion. Cook for 5 minutes. Add the carrot. Remove the flakes and discard. Cook for 2 minutes. Season with shoyu, mirin, or sake. Simmer. Switch off. Dip the noodles in hot water before serving them equally. Pour in the broth. Garnish with scallion and nori. Add the shichimi.

CUCUMBER, CHINESE CABBAGE, AND RADISH SALAD

- 1 small cucumber, cut in half, then thinly sliced
- 8 Chinese cabbage leaves, finely sliced
- 4 radishes, thinly sliced diagonally
- ½ tsp sea salt
- 1 tbsp sunflower seeds

Place all ingredients (except the sunflower seeds) in a deep dish. Sprinkle on the salt and gently work the mixture with your hands for 1 minute. Put a flat plate on top and weigh it down with a gallon jug of water for 10-15 minutes. Remove the jug but leave the plate on. Firmly hold the top and bottom plates together before tipping them over a sink to remove excess water. Place the salad in another serving bowl. In a pan, brush oil over the sunflower seeds to roast them. Sprinkle and serve.

VEGETABLE STEW

- 1 onion, peeled, cut into quarters
- 1 cup squash, washed, unpeeled, cut into big chunks
- 1 large carrot, scrubbed, cut into chunks
- 1 cup daikon, scrubbed, cut into chunks
- 2-inch kombu, cut into strips
- ½ tsp sea salt
- 1 tsp shoyu (to taste)

Place the vegetables and kombu inside a heavy pan. Pour in the water. Sprinkle in salt. Cover and bring to a boil. Reduce to a medium flame. Cook for 20-30 minutes. Reduce to ½ cup of water. Season with shoyu. Cover and simmer for 1 minute. Serve.

Kombu, a type of Japanese sea kelp, is highly nutritious and flavorsome.

BLANCHED SALAD WITH VINEGAR

- 1 cup cabbage, cut into ¾-in squares
- 1 carrot, washed, cut diagonally into ¼-inch pieces
- 1 cup cauliflower, cut into florettes
- 1 cup broccoli, cut into florettes
- 1 cup kale, cut into ½-inch slices
- 1 tbsp brown rice (or umeboshi) vinegar (to taste)

Place 4 cups of cold water in a large, covered pan and bring to a boil on a medium flame. Remove the lid and turn the flame up to high. Add the cabbage. Blanch for 1 minute. Remove and place on a plate. Repeat with the carrots, cauliflower, broccoli, and kale. Allow the vegetables to cool down before sprinkling vinegar over them. Serve.

TEAS TO INFLUENCE THE MIND

TEAS

The chi in tea readily interacts with the chi contained in the water in our bodies. Since we are more than 70 percent water, teas make highly effective healing tools and good-quality hot water is therapeutic in itself. In Eastern medicine, the digestive system is strongly linked to the mind, with the shoulders acting as a fulcrum, or balancing-point. Poor digestion therefore increases the risk of stiffness and headaches. Teas have a powerful effect on our digestion as their chi can wash through us with relative ease. Umeboshi bancha tea is highly recommended for reducing acidity and heartburn, facilitating digestion, and treating hangovers and stress-related headaches. Use it to improve your focus, concentration, and memory. Lemon tea will help to sharpen and activate your mental chi. Sweet kuzu root tea will bring your chi down, calming your mind so you are able to relax and sleep.

By choosing the right type of tea, you can absorb the kind of chi that will help you to overcome a specific problem. Looking at the sharply defined branches of parsley sprigs, for example, you will notice that they contain upward- and outward-moving chi, excellent for stimulating and clearing the mind. This structure reflects the beneficial channeling influence that this tea has on your mental chi. If you want to move down some of the chi from your head, find a little more peace of mind, or give yourself a mental rest, kuzu root tea might be ideal. It has a very strong downward-moving energy that is excellent for drawing chi away from your head and facilitating sleep. Drink shiitake and dried dakon tea to cleanse and clear your mind of negative emotions or dark, unpleasant thoughts.

Hot drinks help you obtain more of the active, free-flowing kind of chi that expands easily inside you. Warm liquids encourage your body to open up and relax, making absorption easier. Drinking cold fluids can result in your body tightening up, making chi harder to take in.

LIQUID RELAXATION
Drinking hot beverages such as teas helps you absorb the kind of comforting, upward-moving, mobilizing chi that expands inside of you and relaxes you from within.

THERAPEUTIC TEAS

To make the most of these healing teas, limit their consumption to when necessary. They become less effective with overuse and might not work when you really need them.

PARSLEY TEA

- ½ cup parsley, finely chopped

Place the parsley in a small pan and add 1 cup of cold water. Bring to a boil and simmer for 10 minutes. Strain and serve. The upward-moving chi of parsley will rise into your head, stimulate, and move the energy there. Best drunk in the morning for a whole month at a time.

SWEET KUZU ROOT TEA

- 2 tbsp kuzu powder
- 1 tbsp brown rice syrup (or barley malt)

Pour 1 cup of cold water into a small pan. Bring to a boil. Dissolve the kuzu powder in a small amount of cold water in a cup. Add it to the boiling water in the pan and keep stirring to avoid lumps until thick. In another cup, put the rice syrup and pour the heated kuzu mixture over it. Stir and drink warm. Drink 1 cup every evening for 1 week at a time.

LEMON TEA

- 1 tbsp lemon juice
- 1 tsp grated ginger

Squeeze the lemon juice into a cup and pour hot, boiling water over it. If you want an even more mentally stimulating beverage, add ginger to the concoction. Stir and drink warm.

UMEBOSHI BANCHA TEA

- 3-4 tsp kukicha/bancha twigs
- ¼-½ umeboshi plum (depending on size)
- ½ tsp shoyu

Prepare a type of tea by infusing the kukicha/bancha twigs in a kettle of boiling hot water for 5 minutes. Put the umeboshi and shoyu into a cup. Pour in the hot bancha tea. Drink warm. Drink 1-2 cups a day for up to 2 days.

SHIITAKE AND DRIED DAIKON TEA

- 1 medium-dry shiitake mushroom
- ½ cup dried daikon
- 3-4 drops of shoyu

Soak the mushroom in 3 cups of water for 10-15 minutes until it is soft. Cut and discard the stem before slicing it. Put the mushroom and 1 cup of water (including the soaking mushroom water) in a pan with the dried daikon. Bring to a boil and simmer for 10 minutes. Add the shoyu and switch off. Leave for 2 minutes, strain, and serve. Do not exceed 1 cup per day for 4 days.

BODY ALIGNMENT

Stresses and strains cause your body to come out of alignment. One shoulder may be higher than the other, or a leg may appear shorter when you lie down, for example. These distortions are caused by muscles, tendons, or ligaments trying to pull your body back into shape. They also affect the flow of your chi and how you feel. I believe that re-aligning the body relaxes tensed-up muscles, tendons, and ligaments and helps them to work better, and this regained balance also impacts on the stability of your emotions.

THE TREATMENT

In my experience, imbalances are easy to test for and treat. Take it in turns so both you and your partner benefit from the treatment. Ask him/her to lie on his/her front with the forehead resting on the back of the hands. Ensure your partner is comfortable and breathing easily. If he/she suffers from a stiff neck, place a cushion under the chest. Kneel or stand by your partner's feet. Hold and pick up both ankles to see the protruding bones on the inside 1 (unaligned). Lift up the ankles and pull them toward you. Make sure that your partner's legs are in line with the spine. Compare the two anklebones, one of which may appear lower. The leg that looks "shorter" reflects tension on that side of the body. Sit or kneel by your

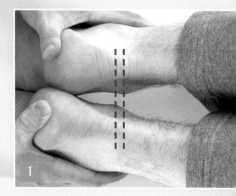

partner's head on the side of the "shorter" leg to investigate the source of tension. It can be found in the hips, along the back, and up through the neck.

With your fingertips, search for the edge of the base of your partner's skull following its contour from the center to behind the ears,

---

■ SIMON'S TIP

These exercises rely on applying enough pressure to make a clear chi connection, but not so much that soft tissue is affected. Practice this by relaxing one of your hands. With the thumb of the other, touch the fleshy mound between thumb and wrist. Make light contact between your thumb and flesh so you are able to rotate the thumb without feeling friction or twisting the skin on your hand. Repeat with the other thumb.

You also need to practice locating the raised border at the base of the skull. I recommend that you carry this out on yourself first before trying to find it on someone else. Place your thumbs on the back of your head and slide them down to the bones at the base of the skull. Work along the ridge in an outward direction and look for an indentation just outside the two muscles running up the back of your neck. If you're struggling to find it, drop your head forward and lift it to make these muscles tense up and stand out.

buttock. Put your thumb into it and rotating it 90 degrees **2**. Re-check your partner's ankles **3** (aligned). If you notice an improvement, continue making light contact at that same point. If neither manipulation resulted in a noticeable change, work both points, one after the after. Observe your partner's breathing as you hold the point for

only letting go of the point once he/she has settled down. Re-check the ankles when his/her breathing has become regular. Both legs should now look the same length and the breathing should be even.

Ask your partner to lie on his/her back with the back of the head on the heel of your hands. Find the ridge at the base of the skull **4**. Make light contact with the skin on the edge of the bone. Imagine penetrating it without any actual physical pressure. Synchronize your breathing with your partner's before channeling chi through your fingers. Continue for one minute before releasing your fingers and sliding your hands out from underneath the head. Your partner should feel a slight pulsation in the lower back.

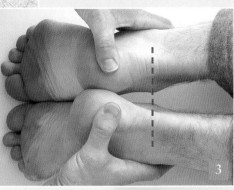

where there is a hollow (see Simon's tip opposite). Put your thumb over it and rotate it 90 degrees and back again applying minimal pressure.

Return to your partner's ankles to see if there is any change. If they appear more even, continue working on the point at the back of the skull by making minimal contact and breathing chi into your partner. If there is no improvement, sit or kneel close to your partner's buttocks by the "shorter" leg. Look for a hollow in the middle of his/her

several minutes. After 30-60 seconds, take bigger breaths to see if this causes your partner's breathing to become more free. As you continue to hold the point, your partner may adjust his/her position or experience a reaction of emotional release like a sigh or a yawn. Maintain contact,

FREEING THE CHI OF YOUR MIND

ACUPRESSURE

A sound mind can only exist in a sound body. If chi gets trapped, it can bring about physical changes that will affect your mental outlook and mood. Twelve meridians channel the chi associated with different emotions into various parts of your body. As I mentioned earlier, along each meridian are special acupressure points, known as *tsubos*, where the energy of that particular meridian can be changed or released. Manipulating the head can free up trapped chi in other parts of the body.

Free up this trapped energy by working on acupressure points that relate to specific meridians in the body. Doing this regularly helps prevent chi from locally slowing down in these areas, which increases the risk of headaches,

STIMULATING ACUPRESSURE POINTS ON YOUR HEAD

1 Push your fingers and work along the ridge just above your eyebrows (E). With your fingers and thumbs, work your way from the inside to your temples (G).

2 Use your fingers to explore the hollows in your temples. Push against the edges of these indentations (G). Work your way down to the outer ridge of your cheekbones (H). Breathe your own chi out through the fingers and into your head to keep the energy moving constantly.

3 From your temples, move your fingers to your lower eye sockets (A).

4 Work your fingers back to your nose. Rub into the creases where it joins your cheekbones. Move your fingers down until you are pressing against your nostrils (D). Press into the indentations to free up dormant chi.

5 From your nostrils, move your fingers out horizontally until they are below your eye sockets. Press into this hollow (B).

6 From below the eye sockets, bring your fingers round until they are in front of your ears (H).

7 Clench your jaw to locate the dip where your chin meets your skull. Relax your bite. Sink your fingers into this hollow (F). From your ears, work along the jawbone and neck using your fingers and thumbs (C).

8 Bring your hands round so they meet behind your head, thumbs on the base of your skull (I) and fingers on your upper head. Work along the base of your skull until you reach the back of your jaw.

for example. Use your fingers to massage out any imprisoned chi. As you do this, you will become familiar with all the dents and crevices that are helpful for locating the different *tsubos*. The benefits include a lighter, freer, and clearer mind.

Below, I show you how to change your chi by using specific head *tsubos*. Press into each one about six times as you exhale to repeatedly channel chi into the affected area and breathe chi into these points. I suggest that you work on *tsubos* from both the left- and right-hand side of the body (i.e. if you press on a point on the left hand, press that same point on the right).

TSUBO THERAPY

ACUPRESSURE

I suggest that you help mobilize the flow of chi around your body to free up your mind by concentrating on the location and functions of the following important *tsubos*. Apply pressure using your thumbs or fingertips to stimulate these crucial acupoints along the meridians in your body.

THE GREAT ELIMINATOR: LARGE INTESTINE 4
(For headaches, toothaches, and the release of negative thoughts)

Press into the fleshy mound between thumb and index finger. Massage the length of the bone that leads down your index finger to the indentation halfway between the joint and the knuckle. Use your thumb to squeeze into the adjacent flesh and keep the other fingers tucked behind so you can press against them. A deep pain will indicate the location of the *tsubo*. Rub this point in small circles to release endorphins, the body's natural painkillers. To break negative thinking patterns, inhale before pressing into this pressure point.

LAKE OF ENERGY ON THE CORNER: LARGE INTESTINE 11
(For headaches and fevers)

Bend your elbow to 90 degrees and locate the end crease in the fold. To activate this *tsubo*, firmly press into the joint as you breathe chi into it.

INSIDE GATE: HEART GOVERNOR 6 (For anxiety attacks)

Place your thumb in the center of your wrist and slide it three finger-widths between the two tendons running down the length of your lower arm. Pressing firmly, alternate moving your thumb toward and away from your wrist until you reach a spot that triggers a sharp pain. Breathe slowly. Press your thumb into this *tsubo* for the length of your out-breath.

PALACE OF EXHAUSTION: HEART GOVERNOR 8
(For stress relief and mental fatigue)

Hold one hand with the thumb of the other in the center of your palm and the remaining fingers tucked behind. Press and circle this area with your thumb to locate a spot that produces a dull ache. Press deeply into it for the length of your out-breath.

GATE OF THE HEART: HEART MERIDIAN 7 (For hysteria)

Bend your wrist toward you. Slide your thumb along the center of its main crease and gradually move sideways to reach the side of your smallest finger and locate the inner ridge of a small mound. Keep your wrist relaxed as you press firmly into this *tsubo*.

WELCOME FRAGRANCE: LARGE INTESTINE 20
(For a blocked nose and relaxing the face)

Place one forefinger on either side of your nostrils. Push against your cheekbones and slide them until you reach a hollow. Press into it. With a blocked nose, slide your fingers outward horizontally around to your ears following the outline of your cheekbones.

EMPTY SPACE IN BONE: STOMACH 3 (For blocked sinuses)

Slide your middle fingers down from your eye sockets to the base of your cheekbones, where there is a depression, until they line up with the edges of your nostrils. Circle them around these hollows to locate the *tsubos* into which to breathe chi.

WINDY POOL: GALLBLADDER 20
(For pain at the back of the head and eye discomfort)

Using your thumbs, find the furrow at the base of your skull. Keep your palms open and your fingers near the top of your head as you slide out your thumbs to trace the tendons under this ridge. Tip your head forward and lift it up. Press gently into the two hollows on the outer edge of these tendons using your fingertips to activate the *tsubos*.

GREAT POURING: LIVER 3
(For headaches at the temples and dizziness)

Locate the hollow between the bones leading up to your big toe and second toe. Starting from the web of skin at the base of your toes, slide back your thumb to the edge of the groove that marks the *tsubo*. Rub it in small circles and imagine that you are spreading chi.

IN THE MOUNTAIN: BLADDER 57 (For pains at the back of the head)

Slide your thumb down your calf muscle to a dip in the center. This should be the thickest part of the muscle, one-third of the way down the back of your calf. Press into it. Activate local chi by pressing firmly into this *tsubo*.

CLEARING YOUR MENTAL SPACE

ENVIRONMENT

Your outer chi interacts with the chi of your mind and, depending on the quality of this interaction, you will find it either easier or harder to think with a clear head. For big and bold ideas, you need to have considerable space above and around your head in order to allow your chi to expand, creating the freedom to explore all possibilities. If a room is cramped, overfurnished, or cluttered, the speed and direction of your mental chi will be constrained, leading to more stifled thoughts and the feeling that your options are limited.

Setting up the ideal atmosphere in which to think will help you to come up with better ideas, improve your concentration, and experience greater mental creativity. If possible, find a large, uncluttered space with plenty of room so your thoughts can take proper shape. The perfect setting, for me, is a location with renewed, free-flowing chi that is exposed to natural light and clean, fresh air. If the chi within your space is stagnant, it will tend to stifle your thought processes, making it harder for you to be clear, positive, and decisive in your reasoning. Similarly, if the chi around you has been trapped in the same place for a while and is slow-moving and old, it will lack the vibrant energy required for sudden flashes of inspiration.

You can even use public spaces to think creatively. Learn to make the most of your surroundings: look around and visit places that seem to exude the kind of chi atmosphere that you feel you need to tap into for successful ideas—it could be a church, a library, a museum, a hotel lobby, or a busy café.

LET THERE BE LIGHT
Spaces with a good exposure to fresh air and sunlight, like patios and conservatories, will naturally be filled with refreshing chi. Unlike basements or dark rooms, such places are prime locations for the kind of clear and constructive thinking that enhances the focus required to probe for vital answers.

SPRING-CLEANING

The quickest way of energizing your mental chi is to improve the energy content of your living space by giving it a thorough clean, overhaul, and tidy-up. Arrange your spring-clean about once a year to stop new clutter and stagnant chi from building up. Spring is the ideal time for this activity as its natural ambience is sun-filled and the energy is upward-moving and fresh.

Places where dust has collected indicate where chi energy has slowed down or become trapped. When you come to spring-clean, take everything out of its place and polish all dark corners thoroughly with a cloth to stir up dormant chi. Remove every bit of dirt and dust from the room. I suggest that you spring-clean on a dry, sunny day when the atmosphere is naturally refreshing and uplifting. Keep all windows open to enable enlivening chi to blow through your home. I strongly recommend that you discard unwanted clutter, as it is one of the prime culprits in restricting the movement and momentum of chi.

A disorderly environment makes you think confusing, unmotivating, and uninspiring thoughts. As you spring-clean, a parallel mental equivalent will be initiated—your mind will start to flush out any lackluster thoughts and ideas that may be preventing you from finding the answers you seek.

If you have a garden or a terrace, take as many of your belongings as you can out into the sun and expose them to the elements. This is especially important with soft furnishings such as curtains, rugs, blankets, tablecloths, bedding, and cushions, which are particularly prone to accumulating dust and stagnant, tired chi.

Once you have taken everything out of doors for a good airing, make sure that you shampoo your carpets, as this is where the majority of dust and entrenched chi tends to collect. If you feel inclined, it is also well worth washing the walls of your home with a sponge or damp cloth.

MINIMIZING CLUTTER

Jumble in a room traps the movement of energy and keeps chi in confined places for long periods of time. This leads to stuffiness, which makes it harder to break out of repetitive thought patterns that are no longer beneficial. If you want to clear your mind of unhelpful thoughts, throw out any possessions associated with this type of negativity.

When you have done all your spring-cleaning, the time is right to consider which possessions you definitely need to keep before you put everything back in its place.

The biggest challenge with ridding yourself of unwanted clutter is separating what you really need from what is just getting in your way. Some objects have strong sentimental value and this may provide an important link to the past as well as be enlightening to your grandchildren. If you are unsure about whether to get rid of something, store it in a box or drawer for safekeeping. If you soon find that you need it, retrieve it from its container. The remainder should only be kept if it has long-term value.

If you can, refrain from purchasing items on a whim when you don't actually need them. In my opinion, it is better to have a few things that are really special to you rather than lots of mediocre items.

CLEANSING RITUALS

After physically cleaning and tidying up your home, aim to energize your living space more spiritually through mental cleansing. Modify the atmosphere of the room by radiating out positive thoughts through your mental chi. Focus and meditate on what you are trying to achieve. Each time you breathe out, imagine that you are releasing positive thoughts to coat every surface in the room.

Ringing a bell or sounding a gong are effective cleansing rituals that can assist you by helping to enhance the way in which you radiate your chi out to your surroundings. As the sound waves ripple through the air, they transport chi and stir up clogged-up recesses in the process. If you feel that the energy in your room is "flat," pick up a hand bell and ring it in every corner and anywhere where dust tends to collect. Keep a hand bell nearby and sound it whenever you have a thought or a feeling that you want to send out. Alternatively, loudly clap your hands as you release quick, powerful breaths to speed up the movement of chi.

Sit or kneel in front of a lit candle and project all the positive things that you want to achieve within this space into the flame. Channel your chi into the root of the flame on every out-breath. Focus your thoughts on the glow of the candle and use its radiating energy to spread your mental chi out into the room.

Just as projecting positive feelings into a space improves the quality of the surrounding atmosphere, so filling it with negative, unproductive thoughts creates a depressing ambience. Avoid having heated discussions in any of the enclosed areas that are special to you. If an argument is threatening to break out between you and your partner, venture outside for a quick change of energy that will calm you both down.

From time to time, cleaning the chi of your living area by sprinkling sea salt on the floor before going to bed can be very beneficial. Salt soaks up negative energy and allows fresh, new chi to enter. In the morning, vacuum or sweep up the salt to get rid of this concentration of negative chi. Repeat the procedure several times until you are left with a thoroughly purified atmosphere, where you are able to think and operate clearly. This powerful process becomes even stronger if combined with meditation techniques, bell-ringing, or clapping sounds.

If you are experiencing difficulties in life and nothing seems to be going your way, keep your living space free from these troubling feelings by regularly venturing out for walks to encourage a change of pace. During your wanderings out in the open air, take in different types of outside chi, making it easier to return from your strolls feeling uplifted and energized.

CLEAR YOUR WORKSPACE

If you freelance or run a business from home, making good use of this space to think creatively and constructively becomes all-important. Arrange the objects that you frequently use for work in places where they are visible and within reach. Store items that you use only occasionally in well-labelled boxes or containers, where they can be easily stowed away once you have finished with them for the day.

Aim to create functional storage that encourages easy cleaning while making useful objects accessible to you. Before deciding on what kind of storage units to buy or build, catalog the items that need storing, taking note of their frequency of usage and the type of storage possible within your available workspace.

EXPANDING YOUR MIND

MEDITATION / VISUALIZATION

Defined as the ability to apply your mind to one thing without becoming distracted, bored, or going off into a daydream, the act of concentration can be further heightened in terms of the chi energy present so that you are anchored in the moment and remain rooted in the present.

Tuning in to the chi that surrounds you gives you a strong sensation of being connected with the world. If you get into the habit of "living for today," you will be able to apply yourself more fully to things without being susceptible to distractions either from thoughts about the future or the past. The key to living in the here-and-now is to find the simplest thing extraordinary. Train your mind to observe life's little details and its peculiarities, and set time aside in which to really observe, investigate, and study what surrounds you in a way that holds your attention time and time again. Many of us find it easier to remain focused if an activity brings out competitiveness in us or is, to some degree, challenging. It is more difficult to approach a state of acute concentration in a calm and controlled way.

In addition to the t'ai chi walk on pages 36-37, there are other ways to attain profound concentration. Firstly, get closer to the present moment by pausing and asking yourself questions that relate to the task at hand. Secondly, use all five senses to help you see, feel, smell, hear, and (if possible) taste the experience.

PRACTICAL MEDITATION TIPS

Sit, kneel, or stand comfortably. Keep your back straight so that all the chakras below the Crown Chakra are vertically aligned. In this position, it is easier to charge all seven of these energy centers with new chi. Wear loose cotton clothing or meditate naked so your body comes immediately into contact with the surrounding chi.

Rest your hands on your legs with the palms facing up to interact with the surrounding chi. Whatever position you sit in, open your palms as this will enhance the flow of chi. Keep your spine straight but relaxed and avoid any rigidity.

Focus your attention on your breath to gradually enter a state of deep meditation. Meditation is an effective but gentle way of training the mind to develop strength, clarity, and understanding. As you relax into it further, you will feel your breathing in and out leveling off and becoming more shallow.

POINTS OF FOCUS
An agitated mind may be calmed by intently fixing one's gaze on an object like a candle. With repeated practice, this simple act of concentration will help to restrain the flow of unwanted thoughts.

CANDLE MEDITATION

This deep meditation exercises enhances the act of concentration using an object, such as a candle, as a focal point. Candle meditation is a good starting point for training your mind for longer contemplative sessions. Choose a location where your eye won't be distracted by any movement other than the candle's flickering flame. Light the wick and place the candle in front of you with the flame at eye-level. Position it so that you face North if you want to absorb a quieter kind of chi during your practice or wish to gently ease yourself to sleep after meditating.

Settle down and breathe slowly and deeply, feeling the full effect of the air as it enters and leaves your body through the inside of your nose, throat, and lungs. Feel the coolness of the air entering on the in-breath and its warmth as it leaves you on the out-breath.

Rest your eyes on the candle before you and observe the flickering of the flame. Pause to take in its shape, edges, movement, and the way the color changes from its root, through its core, to the outermost layer. Ask yourself questions that fill your mind with curiosity and wonder. As you sink deeper into your meditative state, find ways to hold your interest and keep your attention exclusively focused on the candle.

If you begin to lose concentration, allow your gaze to come just out of focus on the out-breath and, as you breathe in, allow your mind to fill with thoughts. Ask yourself questions about issues of concern to you. Probe your mind with a relevant question, relax, meditate on the flame in front of you, and see whether an answer enters your mind. Also pay close attention to any ideas that might come into your head at this point. When you are ready, begin to come out of your meditative state.

Locate an object or a point in the room that is at a comfortable height with your gaze and can easily hold your attention. Focus on it. As your concentration is heightened, you will come to blink less frequently.

Initially, your session may last only a few seconds, but once you have trained and disciplined your mind in the soothing ways of meditation, you will be able to contemplate for several minutes at a time.

SEEING AND INTERPRETING AURAS

The same basic principles that apply to candle meditation also characterize the ability to experience either your own, or another's, aura or outer chi energy field. Team up with a partner for the following exercise. Ask him or her to stand in front of a white wall or background.

Prepare mentally by first entering a state of relaxation using the candle meditation technique discussed on page 77. Start by looking at your partner. Shift your gaze to the edge of his/her skull. Fix your eyes intently on the point where the border of your partner's head meets the white backdrop until your vision begins to blur.

Using your eyes, begin to trace the edge around your partner's crown. Soften your gaze a little by concentrating on a point halfway between your partner's head and the white background. Relax and continue to keep your mind focused on the periphery of the other person's head. You should eventually be able to see a faint haze around it.

If you repeat this exercise several times, or are diligent with your practice, you will soon be able to see the different shapes and colors within your partner's aura and use these signs to understand his/her energy levels. A golden yellow hue, for example, generally indicates good health. An orange or reddish color suggests that the inner chi is excessively active, whereas a blue or green tint is associated with thinner chi in the body.

Observe whether your partner's chi is evenly distributed or extends more at some points than at others. Those places around his/her head where the aura appears to be radiating out furthest indicate the presence of strong chi. This may be due to chi overactivity, a recent release of energy, or simply an inability to hold onto it.

Muddied or faint colors and little radiance suggest that there is scarce electromagnetic activity going on, possibly because your partner is either holding on to his/her energy or there is a weakness. This phenomenon is frequently encountered when the subject is feeling depressed or downcast.

You will need to spend plenty of time detecting auras before you are able to judge what is typical and what presents a possible chi disturbance. The color of the aura around someone's head is quick to change, so be sure to take several readings before you reach a final assessment.

CLEANSING THE MIND

This exercise clears your mind by promoting a fresh flow of chi around your head. Its method first concentrates the chi at the center of your head, then lets it radiate outward. This released energy picks up more chi on the way, before being forcefully expelled through the skin.

Start by focusing on a point at the center of your being such as the Stomach Chakra. Generate a mental picture to characterize it. Hold this image in your mind's eye for a few seconds and visualize lighting a candle with a flame that spreads light and warmth as it flickers.

As you visualize this light emanating and feel its warmth radiating out, imagine each cell in your body turning a golden color as it is drenched by the glow. Do not rush this sequence and take your time over the details to avoid losing concentration.

Once this mental light reaches the skin covering your head, imagine bolts of lightning flashing out from your head and a luminous explosion out into the atmosphere. Repeat this part until you have cleared out all stagnant, mental chi. Don't rush through it though as you could get jumpy and restless if your energy becomes too charged.

SETTLING THE CHI INSIDE YOUR HEAD

A favorite visualization of mine is one that helps to calm mental chi by opening up the Throat Chakra and allowing the chi from your head to drain into the underlying energy centers. Imagine that you are placing your hands on your head. Feel them press gently against your skull. Envisage your hands passing through your cranium into your brain. Allow your fingers to caress and envelop your cerebral center. Tip your head back slightly as you relax and open up your mouth and throat. Breathe in through the mouth, paying particular attention to the sensation of air passing through the opened Throat Chakra. Imagine the chi flowing slowly down from your neck and into your chest or abdomen to generate a warm glow. Repeat this process several times until your mind reaches the desired level of calm. The benefits of this technique include greater relaxation, improved sleeping patterns, and feelings of contentment.

FENG SHUI

In feng shui, energy can be divided into the four cardinal points of the compass—North, South, East, and West—as well as the four directions in between—North-East, North-West, South-East, and South-West. Each type of chi correlates with a particular time of day and season. The easiest way to look at it is to think where the sun is in the sky in each direction. For example, the sun rises in the East bringing more upward moving energy and sets in the West radiating more focused chi. Read through the different descriptions and consider the type of energy that you could benefit having more of in your life.

Each time you turn to a new compass direction, you come under the influence of a particular type of chi so, if exposed to it for long enough, you will eventually absorb enough of this energy and take on some of its characteristics.

The Crown Chakra points upward, which is the direction from which we absorb energy most readily. The most natural way to redirect chi is through your head during sleep, followed by sitting with the front of your body facing in a given direction. You will need to review this often as your needs change over time, and you may benefit from exposure to different types of chi at different stages of your life.

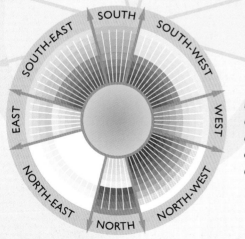

In typical Oriental style, North is shown at the bottom of the wheel rather than at the top. However, North here corresponds with North on a compass or a map.

SOUTH-EAST

Time: Mid-morning, as the sun is rising up in the sky.

Season: Late spring changing into early summer.

Benefits: Encourages you to be imaginative, creative, and open-minded. Helps you be more sensitive and seek harmony with others.

Risks of overexposure: Increases feelings of impatience and irritability.

EAST

Time: Early morning at sunrise.

Season: Spring.

Benefits: Stimulates the desire to start new projects. Encourages greater alertness, and an enhanced capacity to concentrate, focus on details, get things right, analyze, and be precise.

Risks of overexposure: Can exacerbate existing feelings of anger and frustration.

NORTH-EAST

Time: Early morning at dawn.

Season: Late winter turning into early spring.

Benefits: Engenders the motivation, drive, and outgoingness required to seize opportunities, win, compete, and be adventurous in your risk-taking.

Risks of overexposure: May compel you to satisfy your greed by attempting to manipulate others.

SOUTH

Time: Midday, as the sun is reaching its highest point in the sky.

Season: Midsummer.

Benefits: Increases passionate feelings, promotes excitement, flamboyance, pride, and generosity.

Risks of overexposure: Can lead to feelings of self-centeredness, which cause stress and hysterical outbursts.

SOUTH-WEST

Time: Late afternoon, as the sun is moving down in the sky.

Season: Late summer changing into early fall.

Benefits: Helps you feel greater inner stability and security. Ideal to become more caring, patient, and sympathetic toward others.

Risks of overexposure: Can lead to dependency and jealousy.

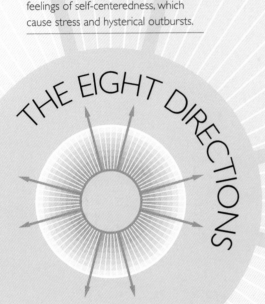

THE EIGHT DIRECTIONS

WEST

Time: Early evening at sunset.

Season: Fall.

Benefits: Encourages a playful, romantic, and content outlook on life. Gives you the increased focus to concentrate on your finances and complete projects.

Risks of overexposure: Can lead to pessimistic and depressive feelings.

NORTH

Time: At night in full darkness.

Season: Midwinter.

Benefits: Increases sexual drive, spirituality, and independence. Ideal for improving your sex life, and for conceiving a baby. Good for boosting your health, the ability to self-heal, and overall vitality.

Risks of overexposure: Can lead to feelings of aloofness that may consequently result in isolation.

NORTH-WEST

Time: Late evening at dusk.

Season: Late fall changing into winter.

Benefits: Allows you to take control in a dignified and responsible manner. Encourages you to trust your intuition and act wisely.

Risks of overexposure: Tends to awaken a propensity for arrogance and overbearance.

SLEEPING IN THE "RIGHT" DIRECTION

Assess your current sleeping orientation using a compass. To take a reading, point the compass body in the direction that the top of your head is pointing toward and turn the dial so the needle lines up at 0 degrees. Note down the direction in which the dial lines up with the center of the compass body. Read through the descriptions below to discover which bearings would most suit your needs.

NORTH (345°-15°)

Having the top of your head pointing North will improve your quality of sleep, enhance feelings of peace and tranquility, and bring you closer to the spiritual realm. It can help you to feel more intimate, affectionate, and sexual, but is usually too "quiet" an energy for a young, active person.

SOUTH (165°-195°)

Anyone who has trouble sleeping, gets easily stressed, is over-emotional, or happens to be going through a rocky patch in a relationship should not sleep with his/her head facing South. Ideal if you are single, are looking to find passion, and desire to be noticed. Its chi, which is most active at midday and during midsummer when the sun is at its peak, is powerful, hot, and fiery.

EAST (75°-105°)

If you sleep with the top of your head facing East, you'll find yourself becoming more ambitious and eager to get things done. Energy from the East is active, focused, and corresponds with the time of beginnings. It helps you to wake up feeling enthusiastic about getting on with your day and can give you that little extra push if you have difficulty getting out of bed. Excellent for building up your life and undertaking new projects.

WEST (255°-285°)

Sleeping with the top of your head facing West is beneficial for maintaining good relationships and spicing up your sex life as it encourages playfulness and vitality with your partner. Chi from the West combines the benefits of restful sleep with feelings of contentment. This romantic energy induces a state of relaxation that comes with feeling content and is most active at sunset and during fall.

NORTH-EAST (15°-75°)

Be careful about sleeping with the top of your head turned to the North-East as this harsh, piercing chi may interrupt a good night's sleep, make you edgy, and increase the incidence of nightmares. This chi is ideal if you want to gain a sense of direction in your life as it drives you to be more decisive, focused, and competitive.

NORTH-WEST (285°-345°)

Sleeping with the top of your head facing North-West encourages long, deep sleep. This mature energy may be restricting if you are young or carefree, and would be better suited to someone older and more settled. Active at dusk, in late fall, or winter, North-West draws in chi associated with leadership and responsibility.

SOUTH-EAST (105°-165°)

If you go to bed facing South-East, you will help revive a flagging relationship or free up those creativity blocks that have been hindering your output. Energy from the South-East is associated with the sun's ascent and spring changing into summer. This chi equates with a time of growth and is useful for raising deflated chi levels, so persevere with it if you want to achieve long-term goals.

SOUTH-WEST (195°-255°)

Point the top of your head South-West to feel harmonious, open to consolidation, and willing to work with people, as well as to improve your quality of life, relationships, family life, and workplace. South-West chi is settled and slow-moving, with points of increased activity in the afternoon and late summer. Use it to help others and to become more practical.

SITTING IN THE "RIGHT" DIRECTION

When arranging your seating position, the area in front of you should be open to allow your chi to expand forward. Protect your back with objects like a wall, a large piece of furniture, or a potted plant. Sit down and point the body of the compass away from you. To assess the direction you are facing, turn the dial so 0 degrees lines up with the needle. Consult the descriptions below to verify which type of chi you are absorbing from where you're currently sitting, and find out whether you ought to sit in a different location to capitalize on a different type of chi.

NORTH (345°-15°)

Sit facing North when you seek rest, relaxation, and yearn for the chance to work calmly by yourself. Northern chi is associated with the quiet stillness of nighttime and of winter. This chi brings on the ability to relax, go with the flow, and is well-suited for finding inner peace through meditation and other kinds of spiritual practice. Known to stimulate originality, independence, and objectivity, this type of chi is ideal when you want to step outside of yourself and observe things from a fresh perspective.

SOUTH (165°-195°)

Turn to face South if you want to feel like more of a social animal, either informally with friends or when entertaining. Fiery, midday, chi from the South activates self-expression and extroversion. This vibrant, mentally stimulating energy helps you to stand out and develop your reputation.

EAST (75°-105°)

If you want to feel more positive, concentrated, and confident with an added boost to your self-esteem, position your chair so that it faces East. This chi is ideal if you want to start a career or turn your ideas into reality as it encourages ambition and the enthusiasm to get on with things.

WEST (255°-285°)

Sit down to face chi from the West when you are seeking heightened financial awareness, but be careful of overexposure as it can encourage overspending. The West is the best direction to sit in when out on a date as it compels you to feel romantic. Avoid it when feeling low or withdrawn. This fall, sunset energy will help internalize energy and make you feel content, focused, and at ease.

NORTH-EAST (15°-75°)

Choose to sit facing North-East when you are searching for the type of mental clarity needed to make decisions that you keep putting off. This chi is best suited to helping you excel at strategic games and will make you more ruthless, quick to seize new opportunities, as well as competitive with a winning streak.

NORTH-WEST (285°-345°)

If you tend to be too "serious" or are over-controlling, avoid sitting down to face North-West. This chi is associated with evening and the end of the year—perfect for when you want to review your life to date and get a clearer picture of where you are headed in the long-term. North-Western chi makes you feel relaxed enough for your intuition and natural wisdom to take over so you feel organized and in control. It also will help you to be perceived as someone trustworthy and full of integrity.

SOUTH-EAST (105°-165°)

Bring your chair round to the South-East if you want to daydream and let your imagination run free—helpful when you want to consider your options, take difficult and involved decisions, or work your way through challenges. South-Eastern chi is excellent if you want to generate new ideas using your creativity.

SOUTH-WEST (195°-255°)

If your head is working overtime, sit facing South-West to help bring down this surplus of hyperactive chi. South-Western chi is most useful for gaining practicality and accomplishing complex tasks methodically. "Re-find" your feet when you take in this grounding, security-inducing, afternoon energy.

PROMOTING BETTER SLEEP

ENVIRONMENT

Under favorable sleeping conditions, your inner chi becomes harmonious as fast-flowing chi slows down, intense chi starts to disperse, and fresh chi enters deficient areas. As energy moves around your body and a portion of it is released into the atmosphere of your bedroom, it will enable you to process components of emotions (especially negative ones) in the form of dreams. If you do not wake up clear-headed and tranquil, there may be a disruptive influence at work. One possibility is that the energy in your bedroom is so chaotic it won't allow your chi to release freely during the night. Make sure your sleeping place is soft and comfortable because dispersed, slow-moving chi has a calming effect and will help lull you to sleep.

Certain features in a room can contribute to an unhealthy living space. Below, I discuss common problem areas that adversely affect energy in the bedroom and give feng shui layout recommendations, practical alternatives, and adjustments.

LOW AND SLOPING CEILINGS

A low ceiling will compress and concentrate the chi in a room and is not conducive to restful sleep. In this situation, it is best to sleep on a bed with a low base or a futon, so there is plenty of space between your head and the ceiling. Use leafy plants to disperse condensed chi; their large surface areas help project and spread out chi. Using table lamps and floorlights will create an oppressive atmosphere in such a room. Instead, install lofty lighting, like wall lamps and spotlights, to reflect illumination on to the ceiling.

Sleeping under a downward-sloping roof will funnel chi toward you and generate a halo of dense, slow-moving chi around your head. Use fabric to slow down this build-up: hang a canopy from the ceiling over your bed, or line the walls with softly draped material.

SHARP EDGES

Furniture and furnishings with pointed, protruding edges encourage chi to speed up in a swirling motion. Make sure you don't have any that point directly at your bed as they will direct whirling chi toward you and potentially disturb your sleep. Close all closet doors and temper the harshness of a sharp corner by placing plants, fabrics, ribbons, or beads in front of it. If you are renovating or designing a new home, round off sharp edges.

FABRICS, COLORS, AND ORIENTATION

Foam and plastic are two examples of synthetic materials charged with static electricity that interfere with the flow of chi in a room. Therefore, it's better to have a mattress made of cotton, horsehair, or straw. Make sure, too, that your sheets, pillowcases, and blankets are made from natural materials like silk, cotton, wool, or linen.

Encourage restful sleep with gentle, calming, pastel colors that pacify the chi in your bedroom. Indirect, diffused lighting reflected off the ceiling or the walls also will soften the atmosphere. To bring chi energy downward, have low tables, floor lights, or candles.

If you are going through a period of stress and are unable sleep, turn your bed so that the top of your head points North. This will bring in more of the quiet, nighttime, winter chi that helps to calm you down and lull you to sleep. If this doesn't work, have your bed face West or North-West, both of which reflect soothing sunset and evening energy respectively.

MIRRORS AND MIRRORED SURFACES

You probably won't get a good night's sleep if you have mirrors or mirrored surfaces in your bedroom. They reflect and speed up the flow of chi in a room, which will agitate and keep you awake at night. Either remove the mirrors or cover them with a cloth at night. Those on the inside of cupboard doors do not present a problem.

ELECTROMAGNETIC FIELDS

Televisions, computers, and compact disc or DVD players radiate their own electromagnetic fields which disturb the existing chi energy fields as well as planet Earth's own magnetic band. To test for this interference, walk around the edge of your bed holding a compass to see if the needle swings. Keep cables and wires away from your bed and turn off electrical equipment at the sockets when you are not using them.

ORGANIC ENERGY
Plants also can help to slow down the motion of chi in the room if placed where the ambient chi funnels under the sloping ceiling and picks up speed. The plants' chi energy fields will reflect the negative chi and rebalance energy levels to create a healthy living environment from which to absorb refreshing chi.

RITUALS BEFORE GOING TO BED

MEDITATION /
VISUALIZATION

The secret to getting a good night's sleep is to move some of the excess chi from your head down into your body. This will help to calm the workings of your mind and slow down your thought processes, making it easier to drift off to sleep. Releasing emotions the evening before helps you to sleep more peacefully without the incidence of nightmares or disturbing dreams. I believe that this is a good habit to get into at the end of each day to initiate the clearing process that prepares your mind for the following morning.

In this section, I will describe a range of techniques to help you benefit from the ultimate night's sleep and give yourself a routine to analyze what you do on a daily basis without carrying over lingering thoughts, regrets, or niggling doubts. These rituals will encourage you to move forward by improving your mental performance during the day.

THINK ABOUT YOUR DAY

Try setting yourself a series of simple tasks to finish during the course of the day. This cut-off point will enable you to reflect on the content of your day by the evening and, if there are unresolved issues that need broaching, look at them from various angles to get different perspectives. Try to avoid carrying issues over into the morning.

In your mind, run through the whole day and take note of anything that caused you worry, discomfort, or annoyance. Congratulate and praise yourself on all the things that went well and were accomplished. Revisit those people/events/decisions that made you unhappy and consider how you could have handled things differently. Identify diverse ways of using these setbacks and turning them to your advantage. This mental exercise will help instil a sense of closure before you drift off to sleep. Do it as objectively as you can.

Feel relief and elation at the prospect of there being another way to do something better the next time around. Throughout history, many inventions were only successful after a series of mistaken endeavors, so this is a powerful way to learn. Become wiser through experience and

SOAKING YOUR FEET

- 1 tbsp sea salt
- 1 large bowl or bucket

If you tend to get a patchy night's sleep because you are constantly having to go to the bathroom, this indicates that more chi needs to be drawn down to your feet through the Bladder meridian. Pour hot water into a bowl, add salt, and test the temperature before soaking your feet for 10 minutes. The water should be as hot as you can stand it. Vigorously rub your feet dry, and head off to bed. This will propel chi downward.

NIGHTTIME DRINKS

Having certain drinks just before going to bed will help mobilize chi down from your head into your abdomen. This downward movement is ideal when you want to relax, settle your mind, and get a decent night's sleep.

CAMOMILE TEA
If you are looking to feel subdued and sleepy, drink camomile tea, which has a soothing effect on the nervous system. For maximum effect use loose, organic tea leaves, although tea bags are also fine. Pour boiling water over the tea and leave to brew for a few minutes. Allow to cool before drinking.

HOT FRUITY COMFORTS
Drinking hot fruit juice, like apple or pear juice, will open up and relax the chi in your abdomen, as well as create a space into which the chi from your head can flow. If your abdominal muscles are tight or tense, it is hard to release the excess chi energy from your mind. Fill half a cup or glass with fruit juice and top it to the brim with water. Pour into a pan and heat to a gentle simmer. Pour into the container. Drink while still warm.

APPLE KUZU

- ½ cup apple juice
- 2 tbsp kuzu powder

In a small pan, heat up the apple juice. Dissolve the powder in ½ cup of cold water and add in more water, stirring constantly to avoid lumps. Add to the apple juice. Drink warm. The powerful, downward-moving chi of kuzu and the relaxing, upward-moving chi of apple juice will help open up your abdomen and encourage chi to flow into your stomach.

attempt to do things differently the next time. Prepare yourself to tackle subsequent challenges by reflecting and learning from your miscalculations and oversights.

Make sure that you perform the "first thought of the day" exercises on page 54-55. By the end of the day, assess whether you've succeeded in feeling the way you wanted to at the beginning. If you have been unsuccessful, analyze what you would need to change in order to feel the way you wanted. Simply going through this process of reflection in a positive way day by day will subconsciously strengthen you from within.

MEDITATION BEFORE GOING TO BED

I've found that the foundation for good sleep is a firm, good-quality mattress. A bed that is too soft or sagging will not support your body properly. A futon on a wooden base, for instance, has the dual advantage of being made from all-natural materials and providing support.

Lie down on the bed and adjust your body into a comfortable sleeping position. You may need a selection of cushions, pillows, or rolled-up towels to support areas like the lower back, neck, and knees. A rolled-up towel is an extremely useful sleeping aid as it can be unwound (to make it looser) or bundled up (to make it compact). Put a towel under your neck and adjust the thickness of this support until you are able to comfortably rest your head while keeping your neck straight and stretched. Place something under your lower back to cushion it and align the area between your neck and the base of your spine. Insert padding under your knees to help tilt your hips slightly.

STABILIZING YOUR CHI BEFORE BEDTIME

1 Lie down on your back on the floor. Pull your feet toward you and bend your knees. Relax your arms, neck, and shoulders. Lift your sacrum a little off the floor as you breathe in. Gently let your sacrum fall on the out-breath.

2 Initially drop your sacrum only by a very short distance and gradually increase the height from which you choose to drop it. Repeat this several times before going to bed. If you wish, follow it up with some meditation exercises.

■ SIMON'S TIP
This method shakes up stagnant chi at the base of your spine. It encourages trapped chi to disperse, prompting it to flow from the top of the head down through the spinal column.

Once you are completely relaxed, begin to slowly inhale air through your abdomen. Focus on your breathing to help calm your mind. Start the sequence for putting yourself to sleep. Close your eyes and focus on the top of your head. Feel the skin covering your skull. Each time you breathe out, imagine that the chi here is floating away. Roll your eyes in their sockets and let them settle so that they are looking downward. Relax your jaw without actually letting your mouth open. Stretch your neck and imagine all the chi escaping from your joints into the bedroom. Gently lift your shoulders and let them fall back on the bed. Imagine the chi being expelled, rather like dust leaving a rug when you beat it. Repeat this several times until you feel all tension evaporate. Stretch your arms out slightly and let your mental chi flow down into your hands. Quickly and gently open and close them as though you were flicking chi away from your fingertips into the atmosphere of your bedroom. Repeat several times to release the old chi of the day. Alternately raise and lower your shoulders—replicating this same movement with your hips—to send a wave traveling down your spine. Picture yourself as a snake: as your muscles slide across each other, they cause pent-up chi to fall down on the floor through the lining of the mattress. Rotate the sacrum in your lower back by pulling your hips up and down and letting excess chi in these joints melt and drain away. Stretch out your legs and imagine that chi is coursing down your body to your feet. Wiggle your toes and rotate your ankles to encourage a free flow of chi from your feet. Slowly reduce your movements until you are in a state of complete relaxation.

VISUALIZATION BEFORE GOING TO BED

Lie down and picture a deep, red sun. Watch as pink clouds drift across it. Observe the solar disc gradually getting smaller until it dips over the horizon. Focus on this red glow as it shrinks and feel all your excess chi pouring into the sunset. Let all frustrations, unpleasant experiences, and disappointments flow away from you into its dying embers.

Chi ENERGY
AND THE BODY

Positive mental imagery acts as an effective conduit for sending and moving beneficial chi to those areas of the body prone to tension build-up, like the head, neck, heart, stomach, and spine. Moxibustion and skin scrubbing will help to treat localized areas of trapped chi, while t'ai chi and chi gong will keep chi moving through your body. Even the clothes you wear and the colors that surround you will have an effect on the quality of the chi between you and your surroundings. For a beautiful and healthy body, choose from a variety of chi-nourishing recipes.

USING YOUR MIND TO MOVE CHI THROUGH YOUR BODY

MEDITATION /
VISUALIZATION

If you are able to project positive mental imagery effectively, you can send beneficial chi to the cells in various parts of your body as your mind focuses on each one in turn. Find a space where you feel comfortable and sense there is good, natural energy, as you will be taking in a great deal of surrounding chi during this practice. Choose a location with plants, natural surfaces, fresh air, and lots of sunlight. If the weather is pleasant, sit outside. Treat my visualizations for healing and tuning in to your body simply as a blueprint to get you started. Once you gain confidence, you can invent your own mental exercises for regulating and precipitating changes to your inner chi.

PREPARING TO TRAVEL INTO YOUR BODY

Lie comfortably on your back. If necessary, prop cushions or rolled-up towels under your neck, lower back, and knees. Start by breathing slowly and deeply into your abdomen. Place one hand over your navel to feel your abdomen rising and falling in time with your in- and out-breaths. Imagine that you are absorbing energy and storing up a supply of chi in your abdomen.

Next, familiarize yourself with your anatomy by asking yourself questions that are relevant to individual locations (i.e. how they look and feel). It is important to assess whether different areas feel relaxed, tense, energetic, tired, hot, cold, hard, soft, heavy, or light. As you visit different parts of your body with your mind, become engrossed with each, one at a time. The more you can tap into this process of self-discovery while remaining focused, the stronger the chi sent to targeted cells.

To carry out the exercises that follow, conjure up an imaginary pair of hands in your mind's eye capable of seeping into your body to massage, soothe, and move chi around. Also create a mental supply of a warm, comforting color like gold, orange, or yellow. As your mind travels through the different parts of your body, allow the surrounding cells to "soak up" this hue.

Remember always to accompany your visualizations with sounds that stir up chi through vibration. This will give the deepest parts of your anatomy a subtle and energizing internal massage using the power of the mind and of sound.

SPREADING CHI THROUGH THE HEAD

Focus your attention on the Crown Chakra on the top of your head. Imagine that you are opening it up like a valve to release excess chi like a fountain sprays out water.

Bring your attention to rest on the bones of your skull. Imagine you are spreading chi across them and your forehead. Picture holding your eyeballs; gently squeeze and release them in the palms of your imaginary hands while breathing chi into them and emitting a high-pitched hum. You should feel a mild vibration just below your eyes.

Slow down your train of thought by imagining you are switching off the lights in different chambers of your brain so they can rest in the dark. Allow excess thoughts to waft into the atmosphere.

In your mind's eye, move your hands through the air passages of your nose, clearing and opening them up to breathe more freely. Visualize the wind blowing through these channels. Relax your jaw and let your imaginary fingers caress your joints to mobilize trapped chi. If you make accompanying low-pitched hums, you should be able to feel these sounds vibrating through your cheekbones loosening up your sinuses from the inside of your nasal passages.

RELEASING CHI FROM THE BASE OF THE SKULL AND THE NECK

Imagine that you are kneading your brain and massaging excess chi out from your skull into the atmosphere. As you do this, feel the back of your head becoming lighter. Envisage your neck being fully stretched (like an accordion) as the vertebrae are pulled apart to allow chi to escape. Imagine the sound of old, pressurized chi being released.

As you do this, think of your neck muscles as violin strings which, as you start to unwind them in your head, initially make a screeching sound. Gradually feel them loosening up and the screeching sound changing into an enchanting melody. Open up your Throat Chakra by making a low-pitched hum. Alter the pitch and move the vibration up and down the length of your throat to free up stagnant chi.

Imagine that the muscles running along the top of your shoulders are gradually melting and elongating as they relax and lengthen to produce a beautiful sound. It may help you at this point to visualize the hot sun kissing your shoulders with a healing, spreading warmth. Let go of any worries and responsibilities and suspend yourself in the moment.

Using your mind, move down the length of your arms feeling them becoming progressively lighter until they seem like they could float away. With your imaginary pair of hands, massage chi down your arms, squeezing it out through your fingertips. Pay particular attention to your elbows and wrists as chi can get trapped at the joints. Use your mind to open up the joints and release stale chi. With every exhalation, imagine a long flame of chi burning outward through your fingertips making the ends gradually hotter.

MASSAGING THE UPPER BACK

Place your imaginary hands on the top of a set of the vertebrae lining your spinal column. Start to rotate them so they swivel against each other. Feel the muscles and soft tissue either side of your spine becoming softer, looser, and more flexible. Work down your back. Imagine holding one of the vertebrae at the top of your spine and vigorously moving it from side to side to create a wave that runs down the length of your spine into your sacrum. Feel each vertebra bending against another to create a side opening from which pent-up chi can escape. Visualize the sound of old, pressurized chi being released. Massage your spine making a very low-pitched "ahhh" sound, then elevate it to an "ooo," ending with a low "hum." Feel these sounds vibrating in your lower back before traveling up your spine into your throat.

In your mind, start to rotate your shoulder blades, massaging the soft tissue underneath, pulling back your shoulders, and letting your chest open up as wide as possible. Breathe deeply into your chest, filling up your lungs each time and expanding them to full capacity. Visualize the incoming air releasing oxygen into your bloodstream. As you breathe out depressive or heavy feelings, make an "ahhh" sound to feel your ribcage vibrating. Allow the outside air to "catch" the energy of these expelled emotions.

CENTERING VIBRATIONS IN THE HEART

Focus on your heart and feel its every beat sending out fresh, healthy blood as energy ripples through your body. As you make an "ooo" sound, feel this rhythm moving chi out through the periphery of your body. Experiment with the pitch until you hit on the note that centers the vibration in your heart. If you are undergoing a troubled period, use these sonic vibrations to throw out stressful emotions.

Return to your normal breathing pattern. With each in-breath, make a hissing sound as you imagine your diaphragm pushing down on the vital organs below, squeezing them like sponges to extract old chi and allowing fresh, clean chi to enter. This sound should originate from the back of your throat or the roof of your mouth. Tighten your abdominal muscles to feel the sound in the upper part of your stomach. Capture emotions of jealousy or anger and expel them through sound on the out-breath.

PROJECTING ENERGY INTO THE ABDOMEN

Mentally project warm, powerful energy into your stomach. Release any pressure that you feel through your navel and soothe tense areas with the massaging movement of the imaginary hands in your mind's eye. For additional relaxation, produce the deepest sound possible from your abdomen and allow anxieties and insecurities to float away.

Turn your attention to your kidneys. Gently hold and keep them warm in your imaginary hands as you tenderly caress them. Make a humming sound and imagine stroking them until they are shiny. Deep-seated fears are located here so use this visualization to massage them out of your body.

RELEASING TRAPPED CHI FROM THE WAIST DOWN

Mentally work your way down your body, kneading out stagnant chi by massaging any aches and pains from the bones in your lower back, hip, and pelvic area. Next, concentrate your attention on your upper legs. With your imaginary hands, get local chi moving as you let these muscles relax and use imaginary sounds to loosen up the bands of muscles running down the inside and outside of your thighs.

Focus your mind on your knees to release trapped chi from these joints and feel the knee ligaments and tendons becoming more elastic and flexible. Mentally strengthen your kneecaps and feel them supporting the whole of your body.

Bring your attention to your calf muscles, lengthening them in your mind's eye to increase elasticity. Stretch and massage them with your imaginary hands until they start to loosen up. Squeeze out all the trapped chi so that fresh energy can flood in.

After that, concentrate your mind on your feet, which anchor your chi to the ground. Guide your vision around your anklebones and then toward each of the bones that leads to your toes. Feel that you are stretching these bones and encouraging the free flow of chi. Feel them flexing to open up the joints and let out pent-up chi. Massage the soles of your feet with your imaginary hands as you picture long flames of chi flickering out from your toes. Release the chi into the distance with every out-breath.

Finally, picture yourself lying on a beach with warm water washing all over your naked body. Feel waves of refreshing chi energy recharging you from the top of your head and then receding back down to your feet.

When you have finished taking your mind around the map of your body, take a few seconds to register an all-over snapshot of how you felt from head to toe. Your body should feel lighter, more relaxed, and in harmony with the surrounding world. Lie still for another 1-2 minutes to allow further fresh chi to flow into you.

MOXIBUSTION

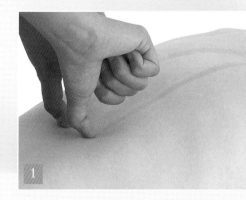

An ancient Chinese method of localized healing, moxibustion is often used in combination with shiatsu and acupuncture. It promotes renewed chi flow through the application of heat to certain acupressure points.

Heat is traditionally applied to chi-deficient areas indirectly, using smoldering, cigar-like, herbal moxa sticks. Direct methods of application include small, stick-on moxa patches that can be lit and then left to burn down, heating up the acupressure point. The rolled-up moxa stick is held close to the affected area, over a point with a particular therapeutic benefit. This external source of warmth frees up the flow of chi into the area. Easy-to-use, self-adhesive moxibustion patches (see inset) are also available to buy. After receiving treatment, monitor any changes to your emotional and physical state. Moxibustion is effective in relieving backaches, tiredness, or low vitality levels, and can be used to alleviate feelings of insecurity or anxiety.

You can use moxibustion on a partner but you first need to identify areas where chi energy is most deficient, and thus the appropriate location for applying moxibustion with visible results. Take it in turns being the receiver and the giver, so you both benefit from the treatment. You will need a moxa stick, an ashtray (for falling ashes), a bowl of sand (to snuff out the stick), a "washable" marker pen, and some "Post-it" notes to mark the places where the thinnest lines appear.

THE PROCEDURE

The person who is going to be treated lies down on his/her front, spine fully exposed. To identify those areas where your partner's chi energy is either excessive or deficient, slowly drag and press the outside of your thumbnails down either side of the spine at an angle 1. You can also carry out this test on another part of your partner's body to see how much localized pressure he/she can withstand.

You will notice the appearance of two red lines on your partner's back which in some parts may swell into broad bands, or appear thin, or may not even become red. A strong, pronounced line indicates a location where plenty of chi is coming up to the surface of the skin. A thin line demonstrates that the chi energy in that area is weak and would benefit from a treatment of moxibustion. No line suggests there is a more serious deficiency of chi.

With the marker pen, label those parts of your partner's back where the lines appear thinnest with an "x" 2, or stick the corner of a "Post-it" note next to these lines. The chi energy in different parts of the back

3

USING MOXIBUSTION ON ACUPRESSURE POINTS
Activate the chi in specific meridian lines, promote wellbeing in the corresponding organs, and address the associated emotional imbalances.

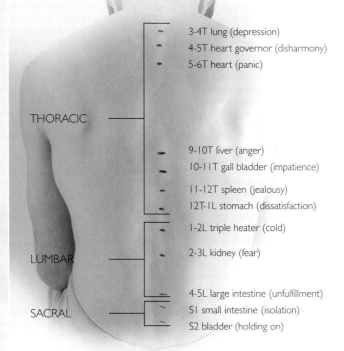

THORACIC

3-4T lung (depression)
4-5T heart governor (disharmony)
5-6T heart (panic)

9-10T liver (anger)
10-11T gall bladder (impatience)
11-12T spleen (jealousy)
12T-1L stomach (dissatisfaction)

LUMBAR

1-2L triple heater (cold)
2-3L kidney (fear)

4-5L large intestine (unfulfillment)
S1 small intestine (isolation)
S2 bladder (holding on)

SACRAL

relates to specific internal organs and individual emotions (see box above). Learn to associate which organ and which emotion relate to which part of the spine. This is crucial if "weak" lines consistently appear over certain parts of your back or that of your partner. The applications should be concentrated on those organs that you find to be markedly weak.

Depending on you or your partner's state of health, one or several such areas may be found along the back. If the line features different weak areas, select the three that are most faint and make a start as thin lines fade quickly.

Light the end of a moxa stick and warm up each area by holding the stick close to the "x" markings 3. Hold the lit end progressively closer to your partner's skin, moving it away quickly if the heat becomes uncomfortable. Continue until the area turns red. I keep my free hand close to the point so I can also feel whether the heat is too strong. Make sure your partner tells you when he/she feels it is too hot. When you have finished, allow the skin to settle back to its normal color before repeating the

thumbnail test. More even lines should appear as chi begins to flow more harmoniously. It is common to feel drowsy after a session.

FOOD FOR A BEAUTIFUL AND HEALTHY BODY

FOOD

Each time you consume food, it is defining and contributing to your appearance because nutrients inevitably find their way into your skin. Beautifully toned skin results from the presence of elastin fibers, but is also attributable to tissues being able to breathe properly. If there is an underlying build-up of fat below the skin and circulation becomes restricted, this will greatly affect your skin's structure. Prevent this type of blockage by replacing the saturated fats in your diet with unsaturated ones; have less meat and dairy products but increase the amount of fish, nuts, seeds, and oats you eat. I would also suggest a daily intake of good-quality, cold-pressed oils—especially olive and sesame oils—which retain their molecular stability when cooked. If you use processed oils instead, they react to heat during cooking and break down, releasing free radicals into the body and speeding up aging.

Whole foods like vegetables, grains, nuts, seeds, and fruit ensure you are taking in plenty of good chi, important when you consider that, while the food you eat fills you up for a relatively short space of time, it affects the deepest parts of your energy field with its chi content for a lot longer. Over time, this energy will filter out through the skin.

Whole grains include brown rice, millet, barley, oats, wheat berries, corn on the cob, rye, buckwheat, and spelt. A diet consisting of a variety of these wholesome foods will not only help you radiate wellbeing, but also enable you to channel beneficial chi into healing yourself, maintaining good health, and helping others. Eating well is a stepping-stone to keeping organs, muscles, and skin supple, so choose foods that contain plenty of flexible chi, evident from their physical structure, which is elastic. The best example is burdock (available from health food shops and Asian markets), a root vegetable so pliable it can fully bend in one direction before rebounding straight back in the other. Burdock brings plenty of elastic chi into your body.

EATING BEFORE BED

To wake up the following morning bursting with energy, have your last bite to eat about two hours before bedtime. If you go to sleep on an empty stomach, your body can then concentrate on healing and regenerating cells and tissue overnight without wasting blood and energy on breaking down and assimilating late-night snacks.

The human digestive system is designed to enable the pull of gravity to shunt food through it in a downward direction. Remaining upright after your last meal or evening snack is therefore all-important as lying down too soon risks slowing down the whole process of digestion.

Since aging results in increased stiffness and loss of mobility, start learning to recognize those ingredients that diminish joint mobility due to a densely concentrated chi content. Salt, saturated fats (in meat and dairy foods), and dry baked goods influence the body's inner chi and deplete its natural flexibility. Saggy skin, wrinkles, joint stiffness, and a hardening of the arteries are all symptoms of diminished elasticity.

We accumulate toxins through the food we eat (even if we choose organic) and the air we breathe. Domestic air quality has deteriorated considerably in the last 50 years as more synthetic materials like plastics and MDF, which contain resins that give off toxic fumes, are being used to construct and furnish modern homes. These noxious particles attach themselves to the body's fat cells, where they are kept out of harm's way. Improving your eating habits, deep breathing exercises, physical activity, and skin scrubbing all help expel these harmful substances by destroying or shrinking the fat-storing cells that contain them.

Be aware that the overuse of particular types of food can result in intolerances that could plague your general state of health. They typically manifest as skin rashes, asthma, headaches, and digestive problems. Remain physically and mentally flexible by exposing your body and mind to different types of chi through a wide-ranging and varied diet.

THE RULES OF ATTRACTION
A radiant complexion, lustrous hair, sparkling eyes, and a toned body are outer expressions of a person's desirability. When seeking a potential partner, as individuals and as a society, we are "hardwired" by both nature and our cultural values to be drawn to visibly healthy people for a long-term relationship.

Try my recipes exclusively for at least 10 days to find out how you will feel living off this kind of chi. Do not persist with the dishes if you feel weak, dizzy, or unusually tired at any time. Include grains, vegetables, and a different type of tea with each meal. Drink a comfortable amount of water between meals to flush out toxins. Eat dishes containing seaweed to help eliminate the toxins released into your bloodstream. If you're one of those people who does not like mixing grains with beans, bean products (like tofu), fish, meat, or dairy food at the same meal, or suffers from poor digestion and food intolerance, combine vegetables and fish for lunch, followed by grains and vegetables for dinner.

On the following pages, you will find a selection of recipes that are beneficial for your chi. Barley soup is the ideal starter dish for feeling lighter as it releases stored-up chi while the combination of kombu seaweed, shiitake mushrooms, and radishes make shoyu broth a mineral-rich, fat-reducing soup. Sweet millet soup is the ultimate in sweet, satisfyingly thick, nourishing soups. A meal in itself, the Japanese use rice balls as picnic food, travel snacks, and food-on-the-go. Pickled radishes contain the kind of chi that breaks down fats and facilitates weight loss. Chinese sauerkraut and cabbage rolls are full of excellent chi for improving digestion and helping your liver to cleanse your blood supply. Shiitake tea is so potently detoxifying that it should be drunk only once a week. Green roasted rice tea has a nuttier flavor than traditional green tea and provides good internal cleansing.

BECOME WHAT YOU EAT
Macrobiotics, a modern derivation of traditional Japanese diet, recommends that the chi of the recipient be brought into balance with that of the nutritious foods about to be eaten.

CHI-NOURISHING RECIPES

ALL RECIPES SERVE 4 PEOPLE

BARLEY SOUP

- 1 cup barley, washed
- 1 carrot, cut into small squares
- 1 celery stalk, cut into small squares
- ½ garlic clove, crushed (to taste)
- 1 tbsp sesame oil (to taste)
- sea salt (to taste)
- 1 handful parsley leaves (to garnish)

Put the barley in a pan with 2 cups of water. Bring to a boil, then lower the flame, cover, and simmer for 10-15 minutes. Turn off the heat and leave overnight. The following day, place the barley, carrot, celery, and 4 cups of water in a pan. Bring to a boil. Simmer for 15-20 minutes. Add garlic, sesame oil, and sea salt to taste. Simmer for another 5 minutes. Garnish with parsley leaves and serve.

SHOYU BROTH

- 1 kombu seaweed, cut into pieces
- 4 dried shiitake mushrooms
- 1 medium-sized carrot, cut into fine, diagonal strips
- 1 celery stalk, cut into fine, diagonal strips
- 1 bunch radishes, thinly sliced
- 4 tbsp shoyu (to taste)
- 1 nori seaweed sheet, cut into strips (to garnish)

Bring 4 cups of cold water to a boil in a pan with the pieces of kombu and the shiitake mushrooms. Simmer for 10 minutes. Remove the kombu and re-use in another dish. Thinly slice the mushrooms, discarding the stalks. Put them back in the pan with the carrot, celery, and radishes. Season with the shoyu and simmer for 1 minute. Turn off the heat. Leave to stand for 3-4 minutes to allow the vegetables to cook for a little while longer. Garnish with nori seaweed and serve.

Flat-leaf parsley is an attractive garnish for soups and broths that are full of dispersing chi.

SWEET MILLET SOUP

- ½ cup millet, washed
- ½ cup ripe sweet pumpkin (Japanese kabocha is best), cut into chunks
- 1 carrot, cut into little chunks
- 1 small parsnip, cut into little chunks
- 1 small onion, cut into little chunks
- ½-1 tsp sea salt
- 1 spring onion, finely sliced diagonally (to garnish)

Dry roast the millet in a large pan until it turns a golden color. Place the pumpkin, carrot, parsnips, and onion on top of the millet. Cover with water and season with salt. Bring to a boil, lower the flame, and simmer for 20-30 minutes. Keep the millet covered with water as it absorbs a great deal. When the millet is soft, switch off the heat. Garnish with spring onion and serve.

Dried shiitake mushrooms contain strong, detoxifying chi, so eat them in moderation to avoid feeling faint.

RICE BALLS

- 3 cups short-grain brown rice
- ½ tsp sea salt (to taste)
- 4 nori seaweed sheets
- 2 umeboshi plums, quartered

Wash and rinse the rice several times and put it into a pressure cooker. Add the salt. Rest the pressure cooker on a flat surface. Put your palm on top of the rice and start to pour in water. Stop when it reaches your wrist and leave to soak overnight. Firmly cover with the lid and bring to a boil on a medium flame. Pressure-cook the rice for 40 minutes. Switch off and remove the rice when the pressure cooker's pressure valve comes down. Lift the lid and transfer the rice to a bowl. Leave to cool. Pre-roast the nori sheets over a flame until translucent. Cut into quarters and lay them out on a dry cutting board. Moisten your hands and pick up handfuls of rice to shape into balls. Press one-quarter of an umeboshi plum into each ball and seal up with additional rice. Lay the ball on a single sheet of nori and place another sheet on top. Roll it over the nori strips to stick them to the rice and press the edges into the sides of the rice ball. Serve.

PICKLED RADISHES

- 8 radishes, washed with the ends cut off
- ⅓ cup umeboshi vinegar

Finely slice the radishes and set aside. Mix ½ cup of water and the umeboshi vinegar in a pan. Bring the liquid to a boil and switch off the heat. Pour the mixture over the radishes. Leave for 10 minutes and strain, reserving the liquid. Place the radishes in a serving dish. Refrigerate the liquid mixture to use as a salad dressing or in other dishes.

Cold-pressed oils, such as sesame oil, retain their full, natural flavor.

BURDOCK AND CARROT

- 1 tsp sesame oil
- ½ cup burdock, shaved or cut into matchsticks
- ½ cup carrots, shaved or cut into matchsticks
- 1 tbsp mirin (optional)
- 1 tbsp shoyu
- ¼ tsp shichimi
- 1 tsp toasted sesame seeds (to garnish)

Heat the sesame oil in a pan. Sauté the burdock for 2 minutes. Add the carrots and sauté for 1 minute. Add the mirin and 2½ cups of cold water. Cover, bring to a boil, and simmer on a medium or high flame for 10 minutes. Check there is enough water covering the ingredients before adding the shoyu and simmering for 1 minute. Switch off the heat. Add the shichimi and cover. Leave for 2 minutes. Serve with a sprinkling of sesame seeds.

WATERCRESS AND SHIITAKE SALAD

- ½ cup fresh shiitake mushrooms, washed and sliced
- ½ cup watercress, washed and chopped
- 1 tbsp shoyu
- 2 tbsp pumpkin seeds (to garnish)

Pour ¼ cup of water into a pan. Bring to a boil and add the mushrooms, simmering for 2 minutes. Add the watercress and cook for 2 minutes, stirring occasionally. Season with the shoyu and transfer to a serving bowl. Wash the pumpkin seeds and put them in a pan. Brush them with oil and roast for 30 seconds on a medium flame. Garnish and serve.

CHINESE CABBAGE AND SAUERKRAUT ROLL

- 4 large Chinese cabbage leaves
- 4 tbsp sauerkraut

Bring 4 cups of water to a boil in a covered pan. Remove the lid and blanch the four cabbage leaves whole, one at a time, for approximately 30 seconds. Take out and leave to cool. Place the leaves on a flat surface with the inner part facing upward. In the middle of each leaf, put 1 tablespoon of sauerkraut and roll it up, starting from the stem. Squeeze gently to remove any excess liquid. Serve.

RICE PUDDING

- 3½ cups pre-cooked rice (70% short-grain rice; 30% sweet brown rice)
- 2½ cups vanilla-flavored rice milk
- 1 medium-size orange
- 1 cup raisins
- 1 cup hazelnuts, pan roasted and roughly chopped
- 3 tbsp maple syrup
- cinnamon powder (to garnish)

Mix the rice and the milk together in pan. Bring to a boil, reduce the flame to medium or low, and simmer for 10-15 minutes. Grate the orange and squeeze out its juice. Add the raisins, hazelnuts, and the orange rind and juice. Simmer for 1 minute. Add the maple syrup and stir. Switch off the heat. Sprinkle with cinnamon powder before serving.

HUNZA APRICOTS WITH VANILLA CUSTARD

- 32 hunza apricots
- 1 tbsp arrowroot
- ½ lemon
- 2 tbsp vanilla soy dessert

Soak the apricots overnight in 1 cup of water. The following morning, place the apricots and the water used for soaking in a covered pan and bring to a boil. Reduce the flame and simmer for about 15-20 minutes. Switch off the heat and leave to stand for 5 minutes. Place eight apricots in each of the serving bowls. Dilute the arrowroot with 1 tablespoon of cold water. Add this to the liquid in which you cooked the apricots. Turn the flame back on to high. Stir constantly for 2 minutes until the liquid thickens. Turn off the heat. Pour 2 tablespoons of the heated liquid over the apricots. Top with the vanilla soy dessert before serving.

SHIITAKE TEA

- 2 medium-dry shiitake mushrooms
- ¼ tsp shoyu

Soak the mushrooms in 1½ cups of water for 10-15 minutes. Cut off and discard the stems before slicing the mushrooms. Place them in a pan with the water used for soaking. Bring to a boil. Reduce the flame and simmer for 5 minutes. Add the shoyu. Switch off the heat and leave for 2 minutes. Strain and serve.

Bancha twigs are relatively alkaline and make a stomach-soothing, relaxing tea.

GREEN ROASTED RICE TEA

- 4 tsp (2 sachets) green and roasted rice tea

Bring 4 cups of water to a boil in a pan. Leave to stand for 2 minutes. Put the tea leaves (or sachets) in a teapot and pour hot water over them. Leave to stand for 2 minutes to bring out the color and taste of this tea before serving.

BANCHA TWIG TEA (KUKICHA)

- 1 tbsp (2 sachets) bancha twigs

Soak the twigs in a pan with 4 cups of water. Bring to a boil and remove from the heat. Leave to stand for 5 minutes before serving.

SKIN SCRUBBING

Great emphasis is placed on looking after your skin, the body's most visible layer, and the one that makes direct, external contact with the outside world. Skin goes a long way toward defining how good we look and feel about ourselves. Today, more than ever before, people are willing to spend a small fortune on beauty treatments to help them look younger and more attractive. The quality of another person's skin is also a determining factor in partner selection—a primitive yet effective way of verifying whether someone is inwardly healthy or not.

The skin is the body's largest organ and the ideal container for keeping your internal fluids at a constant temperature. Through the skin's "ecosystem," body temperature is regulated and, in the presence of sunlight, vitamin D produced. The skin defines the boundaries of your physical body, but can also disclose the contents of your inner state. The appearance of a rash, for example, indicates you have an infection, illness, or allergy while sudden changes in the color of your skin can betray your emotions. Have you ever turned bright red with embarrassment or blanched white with fright?

According to Traditional Chinese Medicine, the skin, lungs, and digestive system are made from the same substance; the better you look after your skin, the easier it is to maintain healthy lungs and intestines.

As skin breathes, it regularly releases negative emotional energy. If this process slows down or stops, acute pressure, symptomatic of inward stress and pent-up emotions,

NINE SUGGESTIONS FOR HEALTHY SKIN

1. Scrub your skin 2-3 times during the week.
2. Limit your use of soap.
3. Wear clothes made from pure cotton, linen, silk, and other natural materials.
4. Use all-natural, organic skin product ranges.
5. Expose your body to the sun for only short periods of time during the summer.
6. Spend a portion of your day naked to allow your skin to breathe.
7. Massage organic almond, olive, or other natural body oils into your skin periodically.
8. Avoid exposing your skin to harmful products such as heavy-duty cleaning products (like bleaches).
9. Encourage skin contact with people who help activate the flow of chi through your skin.

will build up on the inside. This also results in dry, lifeless, clogged-up skin.

Your skin's "ecosystem" is delicately balanced and designed to deflect harmful, outside elements. However, many household products contain noxious substances that can damage skin by blocking drainage and increase the risk of asthma and migraines, while some cosmetic formulas stifle the natural action of pores doubling the long-term risks of dryness and aging.

The skin's sophisticated waste disposal system allows for the elimination of toxins through the pores. During sleep, pollutant-eliminating fluids and oils are secreted through the skin and you can unwittingly lose liquids like this.

THE BENEFITS

It's my belief that you can help keep skin in great shape while getting rid of water-soluble dirt by scrubbing it. Use a hot, damp washcloth made from a relatively soft, non-abrasive fabric that allows you to press in harder during the vigorous self-massage. Stretching skin in one direction then squashing it as you pull it back with the cloth in a back-and-forth action activates pores turning them into tiny, toxin-expelling pumps. One of the attractions of skin scrubbing is the absence of extraneous cleansing agents like soap or detergents that

THE STRUCTURE OF YOUR SKIN

Your skin is not just the essential garment covering your body. It is a hard-working organ like the heart, liver, and lungs. It is composed of four distinct layers.

The keratin layer, which you see and touch, is the skin's most obvious coating. It is made of dead cells that protect the more delicate tissues lying underneath. These are continuously being worn away and replaced by new cells gradually pushing their way up to the surface.

The epidermis is composed of living cells and contains the pigment that gives skin its color. This skin layer is nourished by the blood vessels in the underlying dermis.

The dermis, much thicker and more elastic than the epidermis, enables skin to stretch and move. Sweat glands and follicles (the bulb-like structures from which hair strands grow) originate in the dermis and stretch all the way up to the surface of the skin. Nerve endings capable of detecting heat, cold, and pain sensations are also found here.

The subcutaneous tissue is the most hidden and protected layer of the dermis. It contains and stores fat cells that keep you cool when temperatures rise and warm when it gets chilly. Fat is also a shock absorber and stores extra fuel for the body.

can upset your skin's pH balance. Several minutes' scrubbing, coupled with the action of the cloth moving back and forth, boosts circulation. Notice skin reddening as blood flows up into superficial capillaries to activate your body's chi before pumping it around alongside waste fluids expelled by your lymphatic system through the lymph nodes.

I think that skin scrubbing helps you to appreciate your skin by improving its appearance. Its

brushing action removes dead cells, speeds up tissue renewal, accelerates metabolism, and gives your skin's elasticity a rhythmic workout, making you less prone to having wrinkles or loose skin later on in life. If you live with a partner, scrub each other's backs. Arch your spine while he/she scrubs up and down either side of it.

HEAD AND BODY SCRUBBING

A small, cotton, terrycloth diaper makes an ideal-sized scrubbing mitt. Fold it in half **1**, then again, to end up with a long strip. Alternatively, use a large washcloth, a hand towel, or a dish towel. Fill up your sink with water that is too hot to the touch. Hold up the ends and dip the middle portion in hot water.

Wring out excess water by twisting the cloth ends in opposite directions **2**. Untwist them and fold the dry tips over the center. Fold in thirds, so you are able to hold the cloth by its cooler, folded edges, leaving the hot, middle section free to make contact with your skin. Take care not to burn your skin.

Stand in front of the sink before you start to scrub. Rest your foot on a small stool or on the lip of the bathtub when brushing your leg or foot. Don't perform scrubbing while in the bath or shower as the process can cause a steep rise in your body

MORNING SCRUB

If you want to dramatically raise your energy levels in the morning, start by scrubbing the soles of your feet and work your way up your body until you reach your forehead. The action stimulates upward-flowing chi, which generally helps you to feel uplifted and enthusiastic about life. As this process drives chi energy into your head, it encourages mental stimulation. The ideal time to perform a morning scrub is straight after or before a shower or bath.

■ SIMON'S TIP

The average skin scrubbing session takes between 10-15 minutes. If you are in a rush, however, concentrate on those areas that you find changed color only very slowly, or solely work on your hands, feet, and face. A quick skin scrub to targeted areas is highly beneficial if you experience mood swings, bouts of depression, anger episodes, or persistent frustration. To accelerate your circulation and get your chi to flow faster, grate one tablespoon of ginger and squeeze its juice into the cleansing water. Unfold a towel and hold the corners as you energetically pull it across your back.

temperature making you feel dizzy, faint, or light-headed.

Use long, straight, continuous, back-and-forth scrubbing motions and apply pressure to the skin until it starts to go red. Some parts of your body may not change color the first few times that you scrub. This indicates areas with poor blood surface circulation, so pay particular attention to them. After a few sessions, your skin should start to redden evenly. Open your armpits **3** and groin to work on your lymph nodes. Thoroughly scrub these areas to encourage the lymphatic system's toxin discharge. Prevent skin from moving across the bones underneath during scrubbing by stretching out these parts.

Finish by drying yourself off with a clean towel. For a tingling effect, give yourself an all-over, all-natural, aromatherapy oil massage **4**.

CAUTION If you have any swellings, growths, eczema, hernias, suffer from sensitive skin, or any other dermatological condition, avoid any problem areas or consult medical advice before carrying out

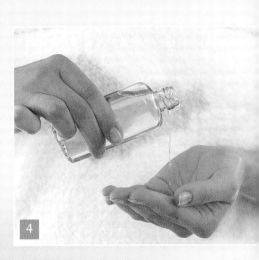

an all-over skin scrub. If you have an existing skin problem, it is possible that scrubbing unaffected areas will gradually come to have a beneficial influence on affected areas.

EVENING SCRUB

If you want a peaceful night's rest, perform an evening scrub just before going to bed. Start by brushing your forehead and work your way down your body until you reach your feet. This continuous movement will pull excess chi energy in a downward direction encouraging it to flow from your head into your feet. This practice results in a calm mental state that is particularly conducive for peacefully drifting off to sleep.

CLOTHING AND COLORS

ENVIRONMENT

COMMAND RESPECT
Wear tight-fitting, sharply tailored clothes in the workplace when you want to draw chi in an upward direction and remain mentally alert and inspired.

Anything that you wear, or which touches your skin, falls within the boundary of your outer chi energy field and, because it mixes with your inner chi, will exert a marked influence on your thoughts and moods. The same is true of soft furnishings, materials used in bedding and upholstery, and those you come in contact with at work. Make an effort, therefore, to buy garments and items made from fabrics capable of influencing your mood positively.

Pay particular attention to the clothing that comes into direct contact with your skin as the structure of fabrics will affect your chi field. Outer garments, like jackets and coats, have less of an effect on your internal chi. Synthetic fibers will interrupt the natural flow of chi inside the body and add their own static electricity charge to your energy field. Pure cotton, linen, silk, and wool facilitate its movement will be more supportive of your chi, while woven cotton is the textile of choice if you want your body to breathe more easily and your chi to move with greater freedom.

Thick, woollen sweaters invariably slow down the movement of chi, whereas tight leather tops, skirts, or trousers speed it up. The shinier the material, the more it encourages chi to move rapidly around the body, increasing alertness and boosting activity levels.

The colors of your clothing, too, can contribute to how you feel and interact with the world. Different colorations influence the way in which light waves are reflected back through the surface of your outer energy field and, ultimately, the manner in which your local, inner chi vibrates. Switching the color of your clothing can trigger changes to your outer chi, which will then slowly filter through to your inner chi, and subtly alter your emotions.

The cut or style of garments further influence mood. Perpendicular creases, stripes, and pleats increase vertically flowing chi to make you appear taller, perfect when you want boosted confidence. Horizontal lines keep you connected between ground and sky. Belts, exposed waistbands, and horizontal stripes spread out chi and connect you with the world.

The baggier the look, the freer your chi will be to meander and find its natural path inside you. Good examples are big, flouncy shirts, dressing gowns, and full, ra-ra skirts. Loose clothing liberates trapped chi, so you can find harmony within your surroundings. Close-fitting clothes with sharp lines and creases encourage chi to flow up faster and define your physical boundaries by accentuating the interface between your inner and outer chi.

What you wear absorbs some of the inner chi that you radiate outwardly. Garments from the day before retain some of yesterday's chi. Especially when you are feeling low, it is important to change into clean, fresh clothes carrying new and energized chi to introduce into your system and lift your spirits. Drying your laundry outside in the open air (especially on a bright, sunny day) lets clothes pick up fresh, natural, surrounding chi that will make you feel invigorated and refreshed when you come to wear them. If you choose to don the same clothes more than once, do this so long as these largely contain happy and positive chi—such items can actually help to keep you on a high, just like a lucky tie, jacket, or sweater might. In a relationship, take in some of your lover's chi by borrowing his/her clothes. For example, wearing his shirt as a nightdress will mean that, during the night, your inner chi is interacting with the chi belonging to your partner.

DRESS FOR SUCCESS

Improve your chances of success by carefully considering what kind of chi you want to project and choosing your look accordingly. If you have an important meeting, your clothes will influence your colleagues' impression of you, and also affect your own performance. If you feel less than confident, opt for clothes with vertical stripes or creases to increase upward-moving chi. Bright colors and shiny materials for articles such as shoes and belts speed up the flow of surrounding chi, bringing on alertness and awareness.

When large numbers of people simultaneously wear the same outfit (such as a uniform), they all experience a similar influence to their outer chi and feel that they have something in common and are bound together. Even for normal office jobs, where there is no "official" dress code, people wearing similar clothing, such as suits and ties, will create a sense of togetherness. This sense of collectivity encourages teamwork through the sharing of ideals and challenges. Because people normally choose their own clothing, their attire becomes a reflection of who they are as individuals. Consider different professions and how this principle applies: stylishness and originality are highly prized in advertising and the media, for example, while builders' clothing is functional and practical.

On the following pages, I will show you how to increase your chances of success by adjusting your dress sense to suit different occasions through color, cut, style, and choice of fabric.

CASUAL STYLE
Loose, comfortable sportswear, such as track-suit bottoms and cotton tops, may be more suitable for certain jobs as they encourage the movement of chi between your body and your surroundings.

WHITE

When worn, it reflects back the full spectrum of light to make you feel untouchable, aloof, and unique. Ideal for remaining separate from everything and being less susceptible to the influence of your surroundings. Helpful for gaining spirituality, objectivity, and decisiveness. Use it to create a clean, self-contained impression. The easiest to combine with any color, but it must be spotless.

BLACK

Absorbs all light waves, making it easier for your outer chi to draw in energy from outside influences. Encourages feelings of integration and an increased sense of exposure to surrounding events. Use when you want to fit in and be accepted. As it does not reflect any light, it is generally inoffensive but can also prove unresponsive. Can be used from head to toe, but it's best to add a splash of color.

PURPLE

When bright and fiery, it helps chi to radiate outward, making it easier to express yourself and get heard. It accesses your emotions and projects them out into the open. Use it when you need to fill up a space with your emotional chi. Ideal for social occasions or for when you want to stand out in a crowd. Combine with yellow for a dramatic entrance.

RED

Stirs up chi, making it more active and faster-flowing. The brighter the tone, the stronger its effect. Pale red or pink encourages playfulness and pleasure-seeking. Red helps to attract attention and make an impression. Pink will make you seem more romantic and fun. Use bright reds when you want to stimulate potential lovers.

ORANGE

Distributes chi flow in a secure manner, so you can work through challenges in a purposeful way. The deeper the hue, the more powerful its influence. Use it to present a warm, stable impression and to attract people into your life. Generally wear in patches to appear less dominant.

YELLOW

As it maintains a harmonious flow of chi, this encourages compromise and your ability to negotiate your way through problems. Excellent for coming across as bright and sunny, but not overpowering. Good for teamwork and networking. Combine with other colors to increase harmony.

BROWN

Slows and settles down chi. Ideal for feeling grounded, practical, methodical, and stable without rushing through things, and for being perceived as dependable, kind, sympathetic, and helpful.

GREEN

Bright shades of green refresh your upward-moving chi and provoke enthusiasm, whereas deeper emeralds project an impression of confidence, composure, and maturity. Use for any part of an outfit, but select the appropriate shade.

BLUE

Expands your outer chi energy field to open up new horizons. Darker tones are more restrained, while lighter options are ideal for being creative and imaginative. Makes you appear easygoing and friendly, or someone who enjoys having discussions about big ideas. Easy to use and match with brighter colors for a well-balanced look.

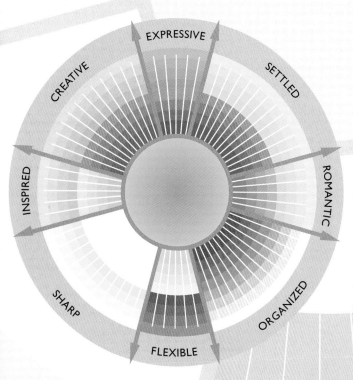

This feng shui color wheel shows how certain colors have specific associations.

TYPES OF MATERIALS

COTTON
An ideal, all-round fabric that breathes well and has a neutral influence on chi. Choose it to wear against your skin over any other material.

LINEN
Exerts a refreshing influence on chi and accelerates its movement faster than cotton.

SILK
Speeds up the flow of chi. The shinier it is, the faster it will cause the surrounding energy to circulate. Ideal for standing out, being noticed, and feeling stimulated.

WOOL
Slows down your chi to help you to feel calmer and more relaxed. Since it does not allow your inner chi to "breathe well," it is ideal for containing energy, but not for connecting with external, surrounding chi.

LEATHER
The ultimate fabric for invigorating chi as its shiny surface accelerates the movement of such energy. It also can reflect chi away from you and isolate you.

METAL
Ideal for jewelry and accessories since it focuses and reflects inner chi in all directions to generate points of intense activity around a person.

CHOOSE YOUR CLOTHES TO FIT YOUR MOOD

One of the quickest ways of turning your mood around is by pulling on fresh, clean clothes that refresh your outer chi. When you come home from work, change out of your tired work clothes, have a quick shower, and put on a fresh set to let go of all the stresses and challenges of the day and embrace home life. If you want a more exciting social life outside of working hours, fill your diary with events that require dressing up: going to the opera, the ballet, or the theater, dining out in smart restaurants, and attending black-tie affairs are all legitimate excuses to wear your Sunday best. Getting yourself ready will help prepare your chi; if you also add bright colors and shiny materials or accessories (such as silk and jewelry) to your outfit, your inner chi will rapidly pick up speed and you'll be the life of the party.

T'AI CHI

The origins of t'ai chi date back 3,000 years to the Taoist mountains of China. This beneficial and multi-faceted art very likely developed as a sequence of therapeutic stretches to maintain good health, cure ailments, and delay the effects of old age. T'ai chi literally means "great chi," its central tenet is the belief that you can expand your chi energy field and use its sphere of influence to benefit and defend yourself or become a healer of others.

A strong martial art element underpins t'ai chi, based on the idea that you can use your own chi and physical flexibility to respond to an attack by turning your opponent's force against him/her. Techniques for learning how to yield, becoming elastic, and remaining calm make it possible for you to re-direct the force aimed against you and turn it to your advantage.

Modern t'ai chi is largely based on the Yang Short Form. This is a sequence of wide, expansive movements that help to strengthen and move chi through your body. The idea is to carry out these moves in slow motion, so that practice will enable you to perfect these motions, helping to mobilize your chi. In this form, you can practice t'ai chi on your own, but it is also helpful to do it with a partner, as this will teach you both new ways of interacting with each other. If t'ai chi really appeals to you, enrol in classes that teach the complete Short Form.

When first attempting t'ai chi, doing everything in slow motion may seem rather strange. Make a point of adjusting to a different frequency, so you create the quality time and space to properly live out your t'ai chi practice. This can be difficult to achieve with a hectic lifestyle, but is very rewarding if you manage to do it on a daily basis. When moving your feet during t'ai chi, adopt a stance where they are

CUPPING YOUR ELBOW

A common t'ai chi movement involves keeping your lower hand palm up and cupped below the elbow of your opposite arm. You do not need to make actual contact, but simply adopt this motion as an energetic support. Standing balanced on your feet, begin to move your free arm in a blocking gesture that uses the forearm to fend off the energy coming toward you. Switch arm positions.

Keep swapping arms. Initially, trying to move the whole of your body correctly will occupy your full attention. The objective is to reach a point of equilibrium and awareness, where you can freely perform the physical movements while staying entirely focused on your breathing and mobilizing your chi.

approximately shoulder-width apart and placed one in front of the other. In this position, practice shifting your body weight from one foot to the other. Maintain one-third of your weight over one foot, two-thirds over the other, and proceed to swap over. Lower your center of gravity by bending your knees comfortably and breathing deeply into your abdomen. When you change the position of your feet, maintain minimal contact with the ground and let them gently glide over it with the lightest touch.

Before you do any t'ai chi, find a space large enough to move around in without the fear of hitting or breaking something. In China, this form of physical meditation is practiced communally in city parks early in the morning. T'ai chi is usually performed outdoors to guarantee maximum exposure to the elements and their chi making the process more powerful.

HOLDING THE BALL

One of the key visualization exercises in t'ai chi involves imagining holding a large ball to generate a localized sensation of chi between your hands (see page 32). Choose your stance and start to "play" with this energy as though it had taken the form of a ball.

Begin by holding one hand over the other with your palms facing each other. Swap the position of your arms while keeping your palms facing each other. As you do this, aim to maintain the slightly magnetic sensation of chi between your hands.

Once you feel comfortable moving your hands in this way, start to involve the rest of your body in the movement. Slowly turn and twist as you move your weight backward and forward to turn this exercise into a free form. Remain aware of your breathing and the subtle influences behind every change in the way that your body moves.

Initially, keep your elbows by your sides to ensure that any movement is coming from the chi energy center in your abdomen below your navel. Keep bringing your lower hand, which is cupped with the palm facing up, back to this location to add power to your movements. Imagine that you are scooping up chi and projecting it back into your other hand.

Try pushing out with your lower hand, palm facing out and away from you, letting your upper arm lead the way. Imagine you are deflecting chi to one side with your upper arm while leaving a space through which to push your own chi out with your lower hand.

WORKING T'AI CHI IN PAIRS

In my experience, exercising in pairs helps you and your partner develop non-verbal ways of communicating and interacting with someone else as you both learn to develop trust in the other person. Working in pairs enhances your t'ai chi practice by making it easier for you both to work with another.

Begin by generating chi between your hands (see page 32), then practice those exercises that you can do on your own. When you are ready, prepare to warm up with a partner. Make sure there is plenty of room available as these exercises are ideally suited to large spaces such as an empty room or a park.

CONTACT EXERCISES

The aim of this exercise is to maintain contact with your partner in spite of movements that can be distracting or disrupting. Both partners need to face each other before adopting any t'ai chi stances. Decide who is going to lead and who is going to follow. The leader begins by reaching out his or her hand and letting the follower make the lightest touch. The leader can now begin to slowly move his/her hands around while the follower attempts to maintain the lightest contact at all times. Make yourself as flexible as possible and move with your leading partner to wherever he/she takes you. The real objective is to do this without losing your concentration, so you need to be skillful at moving your feet while adjusting your position, with your center of gravity stable between your feet. To avoid losing your balance, always rest one-third of your body weight on one foot and two-thirds on the other.

The leader begins with simple movements that encourage the follower to move backward and forward, gently stretching the follower. As you both gain confidence in your movements and in each other, the leader can speed up the motion to assess the point at which the other person either breaks contact or loses balance. Because this is not a competition, but more of a gentle teaching exercise in trust, nothing will be gained if the leader attempts anything obviously too hard for his/her partner. When it's your turn to take the initiative, imagine you are stretching an elastic band close to its limit without breaking it.

After the first round, swap roles and start again. Working in pairs should encourage you to consider

LEARNING TO YIELD

The ability to relinquish control in certain circumstances and at the right moment is a fundamental lesson in life. Knowing when to yield and doing it in such a way that the other person loses control of his/her own chi energy in the process is fascinating and the work of a true master. When someone is angry with you, for example, it is possible to deflate his/her wrath simply by profusely apologizing at a defining moment. Once the initial anger has been dispersed, you can then choose to engage in more constructive conversation and avoid conflict.

Bowing to someone else's apparent strength, whether physical or emotional, may not seem like a particularly brave thing to do, but it can be far more powerful than verbally or physically striking out. Someone who is strongly projecting his or her inner chi is vulnerable to losing it just as quickly, whereas an individual who knows how and when to yield avoids confrontation and is able to retain vital chi. Yielding the whole time is not the answer either. Choose your moments. Learn to predict the point at which your partner is about to move by reading his/her body language and sensing the presence of his/her chi. This is most effective when you can anticipate your opponent's moves and foresee what he/she will do next by a split second.

how contact and balance are lost. Once you have established the reasons, work on your own and perfect those movements that stretched you too far.

As you become increasingly confident with the routine, the follower can close his/her eyes or wear a blindfold to make it easier to focus on breathing and moving chi. Relax as much as you can and feel like you are maintaining contact through your abdomen with your hands simply as extensions. This will help you to lower your center of gravity and maintain balance.

PUSHING HANDS

This t'ai chi exercise allows you to practice and develop the Bow Stance. Stand with your feet shoulder-width apart. Your leading foot points directly forward with your back foot at an angle. The width of the narrower side of this rectangle-like pose should roughly match your hip width.

These gentle, lunging moves are used to focus both partners' concentration. Most of the time both participants will be alternately exchanging pushes and focusing on their stance as they relax their arms and remain aware of their breathing.

Work on developing the necessary intuition and sense of timing to detect when your partner is going to push and be able to pre-empt the movement, so that he/she effectively pushes into a vacuum and risks losing balance. Learning to yield so that your opponent's strength becomes his/her own weakness is a fundamental principle of t'ai chi.

Stand and face your partner. You will both need to step forward with the same foot (i.e. both your left feet). Extend your hands forward with your palms making contact with those of your partner.

One of you begins by pushing forward. Simply move more of your body weight over your front foot and bend your leading knee. Your partner should now shift his/her weight toward the back foot and return the push so that you both move back and forth. The aim here is to withdraw quickly enough so that your partner only exerts mild pressure as he/she pushes. Try to match your breathing with your movements to ensure you move forward on the out-breath.

Once you are comfortable with your partner pushing forward, test

his/her concentration by taking a step back as you are being pushed. If your partner is focused enough, moving forward while maintaining the push will be easy otherwise he/she will lose contact and stumble forward. Alternatively, try stepping forward as you push to see if your partner responds by stepping back while maintaining light contact.

■ SIMON'S TIP

To help stretch your Bladder meridian and develop non-verbal ways of interacting with and trusting another person, sit back-to-back with your partner. One participant has his/her legs out straight in front while the other person has his/her feet pulled back, with knees bent toward his/her chest. Bend and lock arms together at the elbow joints. The partner with bent knees needs to push up at the same time as the partner with straight legs leans forward, and carry on pushing up until he/she is lying face up on top of his/her partner. Whoever is on top needs to relax while the person allows the stretch to travel along his/her legs and back to release tension. Work with each other to get the stretch right. Do not attempt this if either one of you has a history of spinal injury or a stiff and painful back.

LEANING BACK

Sit facing each other with your legs as far apart as possible and your feet touching. If one of you is considerably taller, the shorter person can put his/her feet against the other person's inner leg. Lean forward and take a hold of each other's wrists. Take it in turns to lean back, stretching your partner, then relaxing before being stretched by your partner in turn. Work together until you reach the point at which both of you can slowly pull each other into the optimum stretch. Breathe together to further strengthen your bond.

Add some motion by moving your upper body around in a circle, stretching each other as you both lean back. Repeat in the other direction. This movement releases chi from the Spleen, Liver, and Kidney meridians to leave you feeling generally uplifted.

■ SIMON'S TIP

Exercising in pairs helps you learn to communicate by using your body as you interact with someone else's chi energy field. Such exercises are entertaining and effective to do in the company of another, and will stretch you further in terms of your t'ai chi practice.

ACUPRESSURE POINTS FOR ENERGY AND RELAXATION

ACUPRESSURE

Recognizing the location of a select number of acupressure points (or *tsubos*) can help correct chi imbalances in the body through massage using the thumbs and fingertips. These locations never fail in their effectiveness to restore inner and outer harmony. Depending on your needs, you can either use an acupressure point to increase energy levels when feeling tired or bring your vitality down when you're stressed to promote rest and relaxation.

Tsubos are self-regulatory units, and will calibrate accordingly, so it is virtually impossible to accidentally overstimulate them. You shouldn't feel nervous or inhibited about activating particular points in given situations. However you choose to do it, you will generally detect an improvement. Below is a list of useful acupressure points accompanied by a detailed description of how to find and "switch" them on, and their recommended benefits. All these pressure points also respond well to moxibustion applications (see pages 96-97). If you feel you need additional energy in the form of heat, stimulate the activity of the chi within these points by using a moxa stick. Allow it to smolder over the affected area in order to release local chi.

CENTER OF GATHERING: LUNG I
(For opening up your chest)

Feel the length of your collarbone with your fingers. About halfway across, there is a small indentation. Lung I lies four finger-widths below this hollow. You will find it easiest to place a finger of your opposite hand just under the center of your collarbone. Note the location of your little finger. Delve into this area with your thumb and move it until you find a sensitive spot. This point isn't easy to press, so it might be easier for you to lie on your back and let a friend press into it for you. This should clear up your chest to allow deeper breathing. If you're working alone, cross your arm over your chest. Press into the point with your thumb. Afterward, pound your chest with a loose fist to loosen up residual trapped energy.

REAR GROOVE: SMALL INTESTINE 3
(For strengthening your abdomen)

Locate the bone on the outside edge of your hand that leads from your little finger to your wrist. Halfway down, there is a notch in the bone. Press against its side, rubbing your thumb up and down to find the exact spot. Once you have identified the right place, breathe chi into it. Keep searching for the best angle as you do this, maintaining pressure on the most sensitive spot. All acupressure points on the hands are conveniently located as you can work on them anywhere without attracting attention. This *tsubo* generates more chi into your arms and helps release tension from your shoulders.

GUSHING SPRING: KIDNEY 1
(For increasing your vitality)

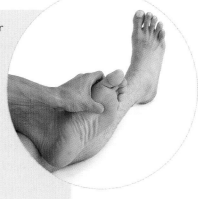

Sit with the sole of your foot folded against the inside of your other leg. If your foot is bent at a slight angle, you will notice a strong groove running down its center. Trace this fold with your thumb until you reach the part on the ball of your foot closest to the center. Press deeply into this pleat and rub along its length. As you move toward your toes, you should feel the bone, and the *tsubo* is located just before it. Press slowly and deeply until you feel a dull ache and breathe chi through it. This *tsubo* is most relaxing when stimulated by your partner. Sit down together on a sofa with your feet in each other's laps for a reciprocal foot massage. Massage this point on your feet until you both feel warmth spreading through your lower backs.

THREE-MILE POINT: STOMACH 36
(For strengthening your stomach and legs)

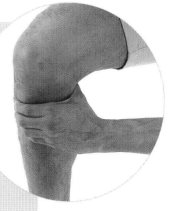

Bend your knee to 90 degrees. Place one hand over your opposite leg with your thumb inside the bend behind your knee. Wrap the remaining fingers around the front of your leg. Using all your fingers, and still gripping the back of your leg with your thumb, press into the groove just outside the leading bone of your lower leg. This is the location of the Stomach 36 *tsubo*, and should feel like it's bruised when pressure is applied to it. Press into and breathe chi through this *tsubo* to get rid of stomach cramps and increase chi in your legs.

LIFE TOMB SPRING: GALL BLADDER 34
(For strengthening your knees)

Sit with your leg bent to 90 degrees. Locate the bottom of your kneecap and move your thumb to the outside until you feel a bony indentation.. Press into it and direct your force downward against the ridge of the bone. It is quite hard to find a spot that produces a strong reaction, so you may need to open your leg up slightly to gain access to it. As you work into this *tsubo*, imagine that you are breathing chi right into your kneecap. If you persevere with massaging this point, this will gradually strengthen your knees.

ABDOMINAL CHAKRA: CONCEPTION VESSEL 6
(For promoting digestion)

Conception Vessel 6 lies two finger-widths below your navel. Place your index finger just below your belly button with your longest digit on the *tsubo*. It is unlikely you will feel any sensitivity or pain here. Slowly work into this point with long out-breaths using your thumb, gradually increasing the feeling of local warmth to the area. When you feel tired, this *tsubo* responds well to moxibustion or a hot water bottle. The results are immediate and set you up for a good, restorative night's rest.

STOMACH CHAKRA: CONCEPTION VESSEL 12
(For relaxing your stomach)

Place your index finger over your navel and move your thumb to the center of your abdomen until you reach a bone at the base of your ribcage. Halfway between these two fingers is Conception Vessel 12, level with the lower curve of your lower ribs as they bend round to the side of your body. Using your fingers, press in gently and hold for a long, slow out-breath. Feel like you are draining nervous chi from the bottom of your stomach to feel calmer and aid digestion.

HEART CHAKRA: CONCEPTION VESSEL 17
(For calming down your heartbeat)

This point lies at the center of the line that can be drawn between your nipples. To best locate this *tsubo*, lie on your back with your chest relaxed. Press into your breastbone and slide your middle finger up and down this point in the middle of your chest to find a sensitive spot. This *tsubo* can be extremely sensitive so work into it gently. Use your fingertip to apply local pressure and imagine chi radiating out from it to fill your chest. Use in conjunction with visualizations when life gets hectic and you feel stress building up.

MOUNTAIN: BLADDER 60
(For soothing back tension)

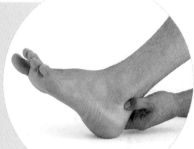

Locate the back of your outer anklebone and press your thumb into the space between it and your Achilles tendon. Lightly press your thumb toward the bone and look for the sensitive spot that indicates Bladder 60. As you breathe chi into it, imagine you are drawing energy down from your back and draining out all the tension. This *tsubo* is ideal for bringing chi down to your feet when there is too much of a concentration of it in your head, or your neck, back, or legs have stiffened as the result of stress.

MEETING POINT OF THE 3-YIN LEG MERIDIANS: SPLEEN 6
(For vitality in your legs)

Avoid manipulating this *tsubo* if you are pregnant as it strengthens contractions and might induce premature labor. Place your little finger just above the inside of your anklebone. Note the location of your index finger. Spleen 6 should lie directly underneath it, just behind your shinbone. Press your thumb into it. Holding down your thumb, slide it up and down the back of this notch until you find a spot that produces a sharp pain. Slowly work into it and focus on moving chi energy up through your legs. Massaging this *tsubo* is helpful in alleviating the discomfort of menstrual cramps and brings more chi into your legs.

CHI GONG

My experience of the Chinese system of exercise known as chi gong is that it brings your inner chi into harmony with the whole of your energy field by encouraging your body to produce its own spontaneous movements to redistribute, expel, or absorb chi and restore balance. The governing idea is that your subconscious instinctively recognizes what your body needs. Entering into a state where your subconscious takes over will allow your body to make the necessary adjustments.

In order to prepare to begin the spontaneous movements that typify chi gong exercises, you need to be barefoot and wearing loose, cotton clothing. The initial motions are aimed at freely moving a specific part of your body without actually using the relevant muscles. This, in turn, helps you relax and opens you up to the possibility of encouraging parts of your body to move without conscious effort. It is important to find a partner or a master that you trust and who you feel comfortable working with, so he/she can closely observe your movements to check that you are really letting go of all conscious commands.

ARM AND LEG SWING

Stand with your feet shoulder-width apart. Bend your knees and begin to rotate your hips by swiveling on the heel of the foot that you are turning toward. Let your arms relax so they dangle and flop against your sides as you change the direction of your movement. Make sure that you keep adjusting the manner in which your body moves to create the maximum momentum possible. Once you are comfortable doing this, breathe chi into your arms on the out-breath. Do this exercise regularly to loosen up your arms.

Next, swing your arms back and forth as though you are skiing. Bend your knees to create an oscillating movement in your arms. Straighten and bend your knees to increase the extent of the swing until your arms rotate over your shoulders. Get into the feel of moving your shoulder joints without the use of local muscles.

Stand on one leg and spontaneously start to move your free leg by tipping your pelvis backward and forward. Keep your knee relaxed and let it bend freely as your leg swings back. Repeat with the other leg. If you're struggling with balance, hold onto a piece of furniture.

ROLLING EXERCISE

This sequence helps develop self-trust and promotes the kind of flowing movements that add flexibility to the back muscles. Sit down on a mat with plenty of space behind you. Cross your legs and firmly hold your feet or big toes in each hand. Roll backward. Arch your back and curl all the way up to the rear of your skull and then back into a sitting position. Practice being able to rock back and forth without interruptions for an excellent back massage. Feel every vertebra in your spine press against the floor.

For a more advanced movement, stand up and roll onto your back. Bend your knees and take one step back as you raise your arms straight out in front of you. Lower yourself down as you bend your back leg and roll back. You should eventually be able to rock back onto your head and then forward with enough momentum to come back up on your feet again. Use your outstretched arms and feet as leverage to help you return to an upright position. Step back with the other foot and repeat. Avoid this if you suffer from back pain or a slipped disc. Make sure the surface is soft and that you have sufficient space behind you.

TREE-HUGGING EXERCISE

The mental imagery of this exercise requires you to picture yourself standing before a large tree with your arms wrapped around the girth of its trunk. Find a position from which you are able to remain "rooted" in this vision for as long as possible. Live out the scene and visualize every detail about the tree and how it feels as you are embracing it. The next time you visit a park, encircle a real tree to gain practical experience, which will be useful for subsequent exercises.

Trees have abundant vertical-moving chi, particularly in the morning and during springtime when this energy tends to be activated. Conversely, in the afternoon and during fall, a tree's chi settles back down again. Close contact with trees will influence your own chi and promote either an upward- or a downward-moving flow. If you are feeling low, make a point of getting up early and finding a tree. See how much of its upward-moving energy you can take in. If you seek the opposite effect and want to feel more settled, do this later in the day as the sun is setting.

Stand with your feet apart, bend your knees, and tilt your pelvis until you are in a comfortable position. Relax your shoulders and put your arms into a tree-hugging pose. As you stand in this position, tuck in your chin, noting any discomforts and making adjustments to guarantee complete comfort. The ideal stance developed will promote an effortless circulation of your inner chi that frees up and lets your energy field settle back down again harmoniously. Get someone to observe your movements and advise you on what to adjust in your posture, or practice in front of the mirror.

LETTING GO

I suggest working on the chi gong exercises on pages 122-123 for a few weeks first in order to prepare your body for the next leap in cultivating the sensation of completely letting go. There are two ways of doing this—standing up or lying down. Discover which one suits you best. Standing up enables you to exercise the greatest freedom of movement, but it might be easier to start by lying on your back—the classic relaxation position. Accentuate all movements by breathing out a sound as you start to move. This release should feel natural and is a fantastic starting-point for free and spontaneous chi gong motions.

At the end of the preparation exercises, practice sparking off subconscious movements by standing in a relaxed position and stepping back with only your toes and the ball of your rear foot touching the ground. Let your foot bounce of its own accord. Allow this to trigger a natural movement by emptying your mind of all distractions and focusing on your breathing.

See whether you are able to spread the same rhythmic movement from your foot into other areas

of your body. Swap feet to see if this helps spark off the desired reaction. The subtle challenge that characterizes chi gong is not letting your mind take over any conscious decisions; in this case, which joints it wants to move in which direction. Do not force anything—just keep presenting your body with options and, when the timing is right, this will happen naturally.

Lie on your back and start to rhythmically twitch your hips. Let them rotate, twist, tilt, or whatever movement feels most natural. Breathe in deeply and focus your mind solely on your breathing, resisting any temptations from your conscious mind. After a while, your

legs, arms, or neck should start to move spontaneously. Once these movements have started, feel free to rest on your side or completely change position. Eventually, you should feel the movements subsiding. Remain still until you have completely settled down.

ENERGY FIELD EXERCISE

This exercise is designed to help you move and "play" with the periphery of your chi energy field. It will involve you "running" your hands all over your body without ever physically touching your skin.

With your feet apart, bend down and draw an imaginary circle around them. Run your hands up the sides of your legs and over your body all the way to your armpits. Extend your arms out fully. Turn your palms over and bring them up toward your neck. Pull your hands alongside your ears and stretch them above your head before moving them back down the front of your body to reach your feet once again.

Trail your hands up the backs of your legs and torso. When they can reach no higher behind your back, pull them out from underneath your armpits and around the back of your head to the front. Bring them down the sides of your body back to your feet. Continue moving up the front of your body and start a new sequence during which you will cover every angle of your body from every direction. Speed up the whole process and turn it into an invigorating workout that stirs up surface chi.

CUPPING

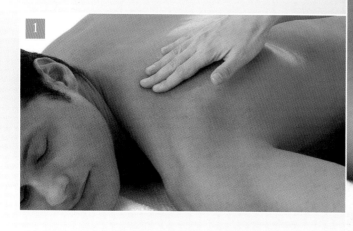

Used for thousands of years in the East, where it still is an integral part of traditional medical practice, cupping is a restorative technique that draws out excess chi at given points along the body. Its underlying principle is to create a partial air vacuum over the affected area in order to suck out chi through the skin's surface. Cupping, sometimes used in conjunction with acupuncture, is particularly helpful for loosening up localized stiffness or tense areas. Try the following exercise on any part of your partner that feels stiff, hot, tight, or tense. Cupping only works on relatively flat areas, particularly those that are fleshy and hair-free. It is therefore not really appropriate for knees, elbows, or anywhere on the head, but can be easily administered to the muscles on the back, the abdomen, and the legs. You will need a bottle of massage oil, a candle, and a shallow, rounded glass jar.

THE PROCEDURE

The person who is going to be treated lies down on his/her front, spine fully exposed. Kneel by him/her and start to rub some of the massage oil into the area/s that are to receive treatment **1**.

Light the candle. Pick up the cupping jar and turn it upside down before holding it over the candle, close to the flame **2**. Your aim is to heat up only the air inside the jar and not the container itself, so ensure the jar remains cool. Be careful that the flame does not heat the rim of the jar as it will later come into contact with your partner's skin and may burn. Keep the candle flame inside the jar for 5 seconds, then quickly place the open end of the jar directly on your partner's skin. If the flame goes out before the 5 seconds are up (i.e. all of the oxygen has been used up), this can signal the right time to apply oiled skin. Then position the mouth of the jar over the part/s you want to treat. If you lose the vacuum at any time, re-heat the air inside the jar and start again. Consciously breathe chi through your skin and into the cupping jar with the help of your mind. Your partner should report "lightness" in the treated areas.

If you are giving someone an oil massage, and want to instil a sense of calm, use two jars. Run them up and down your partner's spine, on either side, to discharge excess chi, relax the muscles, and release tension from the spinal column.

the jar to your partner's skin 3. Do this quickly before the air inside the jar cools down. As this happens, the air will contract, sucking your partner's skin into the partial vacuum inside the jar 4. You can cover a wider area by repeatedly sliding the jar over your partner's

PROFESSIONAL CUPPING

In Traditional Chinese Medicine (TCM), cupping filters out tired chi by siphoning stagnant blood out through the skin's surface, a treatment that provides immediate relief from tension and leaves a sensation of "lightness" in the treated parts. If your practitioner senses there are areas with poor circulation or a sluggish flow of chi, he/she may carry out a cupping session. Firstly, the selected zone/s are tapped using a small hammer with short, fine needles—an effect similar to repeatedly drawing acupuncture needles in and out of the skin. Oil or soapy water is applied to make skin slippery and enable the jar to glide around. The practitioner then places the heated cupping jar over the targeted area/s. The vacuum inside will draw out blood through the tiny pinpricks in the skin made by the needles on the head of the hammer. When the cupping jar is slid across, a thin film of blood will appear on the surface of the skin. This is quite normal and is part of the process of releasing inner toxins or trapped chi. As soon as the cupping jar is removed, any discharge is wiped away. No more blood should appear.

Chi ENERGY
AND THE EMOTIONS

Free-flowing chi impacts not only on our bodies and minds, but also on our emotions. The quality of our emotional chi is susceptible to changes as it comes into contact with the chi of our surroundings, and of the people and objects around us. Explore the connection between meridian lines and specific emotions to increase your emotional wellbeing. Create an atmosphere conducive to successful relationships and emotionally bond with your partner through energizing food, fulfilling sex, regular chakra calibration, reiki, and palm healing.

MERIDIAN STRETCHES

Each meridian line relates to certain emotions which in turn correlate with specific physical ailments. The chi trapped along the length of different meridians can be released through a range of exercises known as meridian stretches, which encourage a more harmonious flow of chi around the body by releasing pent-up emotions, and increasing your capacity to heal and your elasticity. Accompany these stretches with breathing exercises and powerful, chi-focusing visualizations.

● TRIPLE HEATER MERIDIANS

This meridian represents three fires in the middle of your chest. These blazes symbolize your metabolism and determine how well you are able to combine food and oxygen to produce energy and heat. When this chi is strong, a natural rush of energy into your abdomen will help you feel warm, generous, open, and expressive. If this chi gets diluted, you will experience chills and lose the desire to take on challenges.

Stand or sit, and bring your arm around your neck until you can reach the upper part of your back. With your opposite hand, hold your elbow and start stretching it away from your shoulder on the out-breath.

Imagine you are lighting these huge furnaces in your torso. Feel a warm, orange glow spreading through your body.

MERIDIAN KEY

- ● Kidney
- ● Bladder
- ● Lung
- ● Large Intestine
- ● Liver
- ● Gall Bladder
- ● Spleen
- ● Stomach
- ● Small Intestine
- ● Heart Governor
- ● Heart
- ● Triple Heater

● HEART GOVERNOR MERIDIAN

Mirroring your circulatory system as it distributes chi around the body is the Heart Governor meridian. Its flow of energy helps to spread chi into the periphery of the body and is influential in defining the contour of your outer energy field or aura. When this movement is free-flowing, you should function well on all levels. If this chi is blocked or stagnant, you feel disconnected and out of touch.

Stretch one arm out in front of you with your palm facing up. Hold the fingers of this hand and pull them back toward you as you push your wrist away. Feel a stretch running from the center of your wrist back up the inside of your forearm. Make sure your elbow is fully opened as your Heart Governor meridian spreads out chi and you imagine your inner body energy becoming more harmonious.

If you feel localized stress in particular areas of your body, picture them as different colors. As you stretch the Heart Governor meridian, merge them all into one peaceful hue.

● LARGE INTESTINE MERIDIAN

When chi in the Large Intestine meridian is flowing through smoothly, you should feel content, secure in the knowledge that you are on top of everything and completing every task to the best of your ability. When this type of chi is too dispersed, it can feel like you are losing control. This may lead you to feel withdrawn due to a lack of energy.

Stand with your feet shoulder-width apart. Link up your thumbs behind your back (see inset). Breathe in. Bending forward on the exhale, bring your head down toward your knees, pushing your hands up until you feel the stretch in your shoulder joints. Hold for a few seconds. Come up breathing in fully. Lean back as you push your hands down toward the ground. Let your head drop back on the out-breath. As your abdominal muscles tighten, feel the stretch in your upper arms, shoulders, and chest.

Every time you bend forward, imagine you are squeezing out all the chi from your lungs and intestines. Give this energy a dark color (like black) and a deep sound (like groaning) as you feel it leaving your body. When you lean back, visualize fresh, healthy, light, and vibrant chi filling your lungs and intestines. Characterize this chi with a fresh color (like green or blue) and a pleasant sound (like waves crashing).

● LUNG MERIDIAN

As you breathe, you interact with the world around you. The chi in your Lung meridian governs this connection and is concerned with absorbing and dispersing energy within your immediate environment. When it is strong, you feel connected and in harmony with everyone and everything. If it is weak, you can feel depressed and lethargic.

Stand or sit and clasp your hands behind your neck. Breathe deeply into your chest. As you breathe out, push back your elbows while keeping your head upright to open up your lungs. Deepen the stretch into your pectoral muscles (where the Lung meridian begins) by pushing your head back. Bring your elbows together on top of your lower chest on the exhale. Breathe out fully, compressing your lungs as much possible before breathing in and opening your chest up again.

Imagine that your lungs are two sponges, wringing out dirty suds as you lean forward and drawing in fresh clean water as you open out.

● GALL BLADDER MERIDIAN

Primarily associated with refining the chi that enters your body, the gall bladder helps break down fats and the meridian prompts you for action, making you alert and on-the-ball. In abundance, this type of chi could make you too sharp.

Stand with your feet about twice your shoulder-width apart. Raise and stretch one arm to the side over your head. Deepen the pull along that side of the body until you feel the stretch running from the top of your neck down to your hip.

Imagine that you are dissolving feelings of resentment and softening hard areas inside your body. Picture butter melting if this helps the movement. Focus the chi where you begin to feel the stretch and direct it into the middle of your torso to increase elasticity.

■ SIMON'S TIP

Coordinate your breathing pattern so that you stretch on the out-breath to reach that little bit further. It is good practice to work on both sides of the body; when you have completed stretching on one side, repeat on the other.

● SMALL INTESTINE MERIDIAN

When chi energy is being drawn in through the Small Intestine meridian, you should obtain feelings of abundance and satisfaction. If this energy is dispersed, a sense of weakness might take hold of you, making you feel incapable of taking in the love and sustenance on offer from those around you.

Find a bar or a secure ledge that is a comfortable height above your head. See if you can reach it while keeping both feet firmly on the ground. Hold onto it, bending your knees to feel the stretch running up through your arms and upper body. Make sure that the pull is felt in your shoulder blades. No matter how deep the stretch, support yourself on your feet but do not cross them. Avoid hanging off the bar as this will cause your arms to tighten up and you won't be able to relax.

While working through this stretch, create the feeling that chi is flowing into your body. On the in-breath, draw in as much energy as you can. On the out-breath, spread it throughout the area.

● HEART MERIDIAN

The bio-rhythm that feeds your fighting spirit is transported along your Heart meridian. When this chi is functioning well, you will be on a roll, riding the crest of the wave. If this energy becomes overly active, you may find yourself to have an explosive temperament, be prone to hysteria, and unable to handle stress.

Stretch this meridian by pulling your arm behind your head. Bring your hand forward, stretch the inside of your arm, and pull your elbow back until the stretch is felt in your shoulder. Tilt your head back to increase the stretch.

Tune in to the rhythm of your heart and let its beat reverberate through your body. Imagine you have a drum inside your chest and that this strong sound is sending vibrations through your whole body. Allow them to travel and leave you through the tips of your fingers and toes.

● LIVER MERIDIAN

When the chi of the Liver meridian flows freely, you will be alert and active, while an excess of it will cause you to be bad-tempered, prone to rush things, and easily irritated.

Sit on the floor with your legs straight. Draw your feet in, soles touching each other, heels close to the body. Drop your knees out to the sides. Hold both feet and place your elbows against the insides of your knees. On the out-breath, lean forward. Using your elbows, push your knees down. Feel the stretch running up the insides of your legs.

Imagine this chi rising up through your body, creating an inner positive, confident sensation.

● SPLEEN MERIDIAN

Keeping your internal chi clean and clear is the main function of the Spleen meridian. When this energy is focused, you feel decisive, clear-minded, and stable, capable of leading an orderly life characterized by healthy routines. When this chi gets blocked, you lose your sense of direction and experience mood swings, jealousy, and self-pity.

Stand with your legs wide apart. Bend one knee and move your body weight over that foot. Keep your body upright to feel the stretch running up the inside of your straight leg. Increase the stretch by reaching down with your hands and bending your knee further.

Imagine the water inside your body becoming crystal clear. Visualize the sun sparkling off this surface, expelling old, tired chi.

● BLADDER MERIDIAN

Chi from the Bladder meridian is associated with perceptions about the past. When chi in your Bladder meridian runs strong, you will feel comfortable with all that has happened and protected by those around you. If it turns weak, you will be constantly

worrying about what others are plotting behind your back.

Sit on the floor with your legs straight or stand with your feet together. On the out-breath, lean forward and touch your ankles or toes. Pull yourself forward, increasing the stretch down the backs of your legs, your knees straight. Let your head drop forward and feel the stretch all the way up to the back of your head.

Imagine you are floating in warm, salty water. Wallow in the sensation that you are being supported and protected. Let the water dissolve any fears and wash away past insecurities.

● KIDNEY MERIDIAN

Your Kidney meridian chi provides your life's vitality. It is associated with sexual desire and individual drive. The presence of this energy allows you to be courageous, adventurous, and a challenge-taker. If it becomes weak, you may develop unnatural fears and insecurities, increasing the risk of continuous fretting.

Stand with your feet apart. Gradually separate them out further and further, beyond hip-width, until you feel the stretch running up the insides of your legs. Bend your upper body forward and support yourself by placing your hands on the ground. Let your body drop down as far as is comfortable to get the stretch to reach the Kidney meridian.

Visualize a colorful, warm, strong sensation in your lower back. Imagine the sun shining on your lower back and drenching it with energy. Return your upper body to an upright position. Put your hands over your lower back to transmit additional energy.

● STOMACH MERIDIAN

The chi contained along the Stomach meridian represents your hunger for life. When it is working well, this chi gives you the necessary energy to make your way in the world, whether this means finding employment or working your way up the corporate ladder. If this energy becomes too strong, you may find yourself unable to let go and you could become obsessed about work and money.

Tuck your toes and kneel down. Using your arms or elbows for support, slowly lean back and lie down on your back with your legs folded by your sides.

If you find this difficult to do, avoid forcing any movements and lie back on some cushions instead. Stretch your arms over your head to feel a powerful stretch running all the way up from your knees into your chest.

Imagine a big, colorful entrance opening up before you: beyond it are all the things that you strive for in life; move forward to discover new challenges.

CREATING AN ATMOSPHERE FOR SUCCESSFUL RELATIONSHIPS

PEOPLE

To understand why we attach so much importance to relationships, we must first look at how they work. Relationships are a great source of happiness and misery in our lives, and people seek my advice at both ends of the relationship spectrum—either because they want to be attached to someone, or wish to get away from a partner who makes them miserable.

Human beings needed to form good, stable relationships from birth if they were to survive. In terms of evolution, communities where men and women formed long-term partnerships proved better for rearing offspring than those where the responsibility fell on a single parent. Society further reinforced this biological necessity—to rear strong, healthy children who could later provide for weaker or aging family members.

Contemporary couples differ markedly from those in earlier eras. Nowadays there is no real imperative to produce children to ensure you are cared for in old age—pensions go some way toward looking after people when they're elderly. Added to this is the economic reality that you are better off financially not having children. As sex discrimination wanes and men and women come to enjoy increasingly equal opportunities in the workplace, the male-breadwinner, female-homemaker pattern has diminished and with it the emphasis on the family, home, and stability.

Basic survival no longer hinges on being one half of a couple and many individuals prefer to live on their own or can afford to engage in a long line of casual, disposable relationships without making major commitments. Consequently, relationship dynamics have undergone considerable transformation. Emotional pain aside, it has never been easier to break up because there are less economic and social implications for staying together.

Whereas our evolutionary hardwiring is programmed to compel our species to want to start a biological family in the interests of survival of the species, the psychological reasons for wanting to bond with another are more complex: we all want to love and be loved in return, and we enjoy the greater security of being part of a couple. Moreover, two people can achieve more than the sum of their individual efforts when they work well as a team. This is why I think people are still eager to be in relationships.

YOUR IDEAL PARTNER

The challenges that we all face are knowing what we really want from a relationship and what we are prepared to give up in order to make it work. Place the following benefits in their order of importance to you and compare them to a list drawn up by your partner. If there are differences, note them and see how you can both satisfy each other. It is important that the chi (or chemistry) between you and your lover works in harmony. The quality of the interaction between your chi and that of your partner makes a significant difference to how well the relationship works out (or doesn't).

Affection	To touch and be touched.
Companionship	To know that someone shares your interests.
Friendship	Feeling that someone respects you and wants to be a part of your life.
Fun	Having a laugh together.
Love	The feelings of being in love and being loved.
Security	Sharing problems and knowing that you can rely on another.
Sex	Physical pleasures.
Social life	Having mutual friends and going out together.
Support	Knowing someone is there when you feel down or are ill.
Teamwork	Doing things together and helping each other get ahead.

CHI IN RELATIONSHIPS

I believe that, when two people are frequently together, they create a living dynamic specific to their relationship. The more intimate they are, the greater the amount of chi that they share. Once you begin to dedicate the majority of your time to someone else, your chi energy will inevitably mix in with his/hers. During sex, when you share the same bed, or when you spend time doing things together, your chi energy will change as it comes to be influenced by that of your partner or lover. You'll gradually become aware that the presence of this other person makes you feel and think a certain way.

People in long-term relationships come to resemble and behave like each other. When their chi energies merge together well, this becomes the driving force of the relationship. Outside forces, such as the energy in the home, also can influence both partners' energy fields and that of the relationship.

The quality of outside chi can be regulated by feng shui practices. For example, take something belonging to your lover (like a lock of his/her hair) and keep this object close to you. Ensure you select an item used or touched frequently by your partner and one which your partner usually keeps within range of his/her energy field such as an article of clothing, a piece of jewelry, or a watch. Sharing material possessions speeds up the process of getting to know one another and helps to establish a sense of intimacy. Wearing something of your lover's against your skin will bring some of his/her chi into your own energy field. This is comforting if you are apart for extended periods of time. I recommend that you keep your toothbrushes, hairbrushes, and shoes together; when storing clothes, mix items from both your wardrobes. Keep photographs of the pair of you having fun together around the house to reinforce feelings of togetherness and of sharing.

FENG SHUI AND YOUR HOME

Increase your chances of having harmonious and satisfying relationships by creating a soft, calm, and stress-free atmosphere where both partners can iron out their differences. A happy home is one with plenty of natural light, sunshine, and fresh air. After an argument with your lover, open all the windows and clean your house to refresh the surrounding chi.

BONDING THROUGH FOOD

Hunger for food and desire for sex are primal instincts of self-preservation within our species—an ideal mix for getting in touch with our deepest, most hidden needs.

Invite someone that you find attractive, or are involved with, for a cozy meal. If you propose to eat at home, you will be more in control of the environment, the lighting, the seating arrangement, and the menu on offer than if you eat out. Share your food by eating from a single serving dish (or the same pot) to establish a sense of complicity and intimacy. This culinary tradition is common among Eastern cultures, whose cuisines dictate that dishes be shared using chopsticks. Sharing food (and chi energy) in this way will encourage you and your partner to interact with each other in close proximity. This practice reiterates the value of the traditional family meal (now sadly outmoded), originally devised to provide family members with regular occasions in which to sit down, share the same food and energy, and bond. In large cities, where the majority of people tend to eat separately or alone, a greater polarity exists between individuals, making it harder for people to connect with one another through the ritual of food.

Those areas where chi is compressed, moving too quickly, or confined, increase the probability of conflict. During an argument, the chi projected by you and your partner will radiate out, contaminating the surrounding atmosphere, and possibly prolonging trauma. If this occurs regularly, you may end up living somewhere where arguments are more likely to happen.

To avert this, walk around your home checking for sharp corners as these direct fast-flowing chi into the rooms they point to, creating areas of tension. This is particularly important in the bedroom, where any edges pointing in the direction of your bed will expose you both to quick, swirling chi while you sleep. To dampen down this turbulence, keep all closet or cupboard doors closed and any sharp corners on walls or furniture covered by leafy plants. Plants radiate healthy chi, clean the air, absorb sounds, and create a natural atmosphere all-round. Alternatively, drape the corners with strings of beads.

Use diffused lighting, table lights, and candles to reflect light off the walls or ceiling and create an even gentler atmosphere. Candles produce a soft, warm light that helps you to feel romantic or passionate, especially in the bedroom. Table lamps, especially those with cloth lampshades, bring the chi in a room closer to the ground, making it easier to relax and focus on your lover. Low chairs, big cushions, and beanbags engender a mood for love. Direct lighting is ideal for generating an exciting, vibrant environment, but is not advisable for bringing energy levels down and creating greater intimacy.

Introduce a variety of natural materials into your home to keep the surrounding chi fresh and invigorating. Intimate objects like clothing, soft furnishings, and upholstery should be made from natural fabrics. Large surfaces, such as flooring, need to be considered carefully: stone, wood, or wool carperts are the recommended choices.

REIKI

The Japanese system of palm healing, known as reiki, focuses the innate ability of the individual to channel his/her inner chi energy either into the healer's body, or that of a partner to help improve the movement of localized chi in particular areas. One technique fits all and you repeat the same movement using your hands over and over again. If the chi in your palms is generally healthy, it will bring the energy of any animal, person, or living being that comes into contact with your hands into balance. Reiki improves the physical state of localized chi, regardless of whether it is moving fast, slow, up, down, or is too compressed, dispersed, expanded, or contracted.

I would recommend training to become a reiki master to help yourself acquire and develop control of your chi. The inherent belief is that the teacher passes on something of his/her healing energy to the student who, in turn, will help others become reiki healers. It is my belief that the benefits from reiki can be felt immediately and human beings already have a natural inclination to engage in this kind of technique. Putting a hand over an aching stomach, or holding a throbbing head, are instinctive and commonplace reactions to pain. These movements, however, are bound to become more powerful if you can train your mind to focus fully on the transfer of chi through your hands. Although, when feeling unwell, it is admittedly difficult to perform reiki on yourself; relax and let someone else do the healing.

In my experience, the more you come to refine your practice, the more well-directed your approach will become, and the greater the benefits from receiving the chi of the treatment. When you practice, intuitively home in on tense areas, create a longer sequence, or simply combine reiki with other elements of wellbeing.

HOW DOES REIKI WORK?

The life force known as chi flows through our physical body through chakras and meridians to nourish cells, tissues, and organs. It also wraps us in a field of energy we call our aura. Chi energy responds to the quality of thoughts and feelings. It becomes disrupted when we accept, consciously or unconsciously, negative thoughts or feelings about ourselves, which cause disruptions to our inner flow of chi when they attach themselves to the energy field of our physical body.

During reiki, healing occurs as flowing chi is encouraged to pass through the depleted parts of a person's energy field charging them with additional positive energy in order to raise their activity levels and cause excess energy to break apart and fall away. In so doing, reiki clears, straightens, and heals all energy pathways to allow chi to flow in a healthy and natural way.

I find that when I give treatment for me it becomes a meditative process where I focus on bringing fresh chi into myself that I then pass on to the person receiving it. The end result is that I am left feeling tranquil, energized, and clear-minded while the other person benefits from a fresh intake of chi. So far, I have not had the experience of taking in the other person's energy in a negative way.

THE PROCEDURE

Find a quiet place indoors or a secluded space outdoors with good exposure to fresh air, natural light, and sunshine. If you're in a closed room, ensure there is plenty of available space (so as not to confine your chi) because clutter tends to stifle its movement. If you perform reiki outside, choose a location where chi is reasonably contained—near a tree, in the grass, or by the bushes. If you want the treatment to be particularly refreshing, sit by a river bank, where the moving water will keep on renewing the surrounding chi.

When a person receives any type of therapeutic treatment, the individual's body temperature drops as he/she enters a state of relaxation. It is therefore important to find a space that is warm and to have blankets handy with which to wrap up any parts of your partner's body on which you are not working. The recipient should be wearing pure cotton garments; the presence of synthetic materials makes establishing a good chi connection quite challenging. Complete the session in silence to fully concentrate on transferring chi into your partner. Explain how reiki works and what your partner can expect beforehand.

Place your hands over several points of your partner's body to promote overall healing. You may need to dedicate extra time to treating certain areas as his/her local chi tends to warm up more slowly. Lightly place your palms on your partner, concentrate on your breathing, and imagine you are projecting chi deeply into his/her body. Contact should be minimal—just the weight of your hands. Do not apply pressure or lean on your palms. Sit close to your partner with your shoulders comfortably close to the area that you are treating. Let your upper arms hang down from your shoulders with your forearms straight in front of you. As chi gets successfully channeled, your palms will start to warm up. Now move to another part of your partner's body and repeat. Keep your body straight and your head held high. This posture allows chi to filter through the chakras and project down from your arms into your palms.

■ SIMON'S TIP

To remain focused during a reiki session, keep asking questions about your partner, including how he/she is breathing, what his/her body temperature is like, and the nature of his/her posture.

PRACTICING REIKI

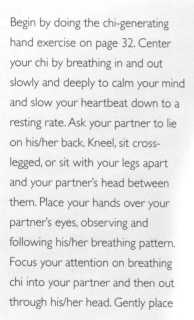

Begin by doing the chi-generating hand exercise on page 32. Center your chi by breathing in and out slowly and deeply to calm your mind and slow your heartbeat down to a resting rate. Ask your partner to lie on his/her back. Kneel, sit cross-legged, or sit with your legs apart and your partner's head between them. Place your hands over your partner's eyes, observing and following his/her breathing pattern. Focus your attention on breathing chi into your partner and then out through his/her head. Gently place your hands on the sides of your partner's neck and jaw alongside his/her ears **1**. Try not to breathe into your partner's face as you lean forward. Once you have found the ideal position, relax and return to focusing on your breathing. Maintain contact with your chi by momentarily keeping your hands close to your partner. Occasionally raise your palms to detect whether there is a magnetic connection. Once you feel heat building up in your palms, move to the next location by slowly taking your hands away. Imagine you are breathing chi deep into your partner's body as this will encourage a more powerful flow than just to the surface.

Put your hands on your partner's upper chest **2**. This area should feel free and light. Heaviness or tightness could indicate pent-up feelings. Lean forward with your elbows on your knees and apply the lightest touch. Observe and tune in to your partner's breathing again.

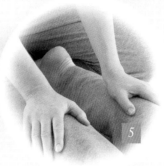
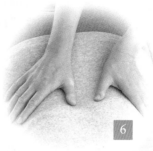

Bring your partner's arms out to 90 degrees to his/her body. Rest your hands on his/her shoulders and upper arms 3. Once you feel the local chi change, move your hands to his/her elbows and forearms. Kneel next to your partner's hip and face his/her head. Lay your hands on your partner's abdomen and observe his/her breathing. Use this rhythm to dictate your own breathing of chi. Move back into a position that allows you to rest your hands on your partner's hips and upper legs.

Sit with your partner's feet between your legs 4. As you continue to breathe in chi, lean forward and place your hands over the feet. Lift them very slowly and move on only when your hands have become warm.

Ask your partner to turn over. Lean forward and rest your hands on his/her calf muscles 5. To allow your chi to flow more freely, lean on your legs with your elbows. Change position and kneel by your

partner's legs with your hands on his/her upper legs. Kneel by your partner's knees and place your hands on his/her upper legs to channel your chi until your palms have warmed up.

Rest your hands on your partner's lower back 6 before moving on to his/her upper arms and eventually his/her upper back. Reconnect with your partner's breathing and try to get a sense of his/her current emotional state. Compare it with what he/she seemed to be feeling when you previously had your hands over his/her lungs. Assess whether any change has taken place.

Position your hands over the back of your partner's head 7. Breathe in and start to project calming chi. Finish by slowly lifting your hands away from his/her head. Keep

breathing chi and hold your palms close before moving them away. Let your partner relax in silence to get his/her chi to settle down.

FINE-TUNING YOUR CHAKRAS

CHAKRAS

In the body, there are areas of intense activity where concentrated chi energy swirls around in a spiral. These are the chakras—energy centers that store, direct, and control your inner chi. The circling swing of a pendulum held over different parts of the body indicates their respective locations (see pages 44-45). All seven chakras are interconnected by 14 meridians through which energy is distributed to the rest of the body. In my opinion, the most significant movement of chi takes place along the central channel that intersects all of these energy centers. At the top end of this conduit, chi enters and leaves through the Crown Chakra at the top of the head. At the bottom end, chi escapes from underneath the torso via the Sex Chakra.

The chi entering the Crown Chakra comes from the sky overhead and effectively establishes your connection with the universe, and the chi coming in through your Sex Chakra links you to the earth below. When you are in a standing position, your body becomes an antenna between the chi of the earth and that of the universe. As the upward-moving chi from the earth and the downward-moving chi from the universe meet within each chakra, energy combines and swirls. This eddying chi is expelled in a spiraling movement that allows the whole of the body to be "touched" by both the chi from mother Earth and that of the cosmos.

In Eastern philosophy, these two complimentary, yet opposite, energies symbolize everything in life. The chi of the earth originates from concentrated energy emanating from the core of the planet, which rapidly expands once it enters the atmosphere. This chi is the life force of our planet that courses through the cells in our bodies to nourish them with a physically supportive, nurturing, and motherly type of chi. Energy from the universe starts out fully expanded and dispersed, but becomes increasingly concentrated as it gravitates toward planet Earth. It travels toward the planet's core carrying information about the universe, including chi from the past and the future, other planets, and other life forms. As it spirals through our bodies, it feeds all cells with information that inspires us and creates the feeling that there are forces in the universe bigger than ourselves. This realization can result in religious beliefs, spiritual pursuits, or a desire to expand familiar horizons.

Life flourishes wherever these two energies meet—mostly frequently close to the surface of planet Earth, where each type of chi undergoes a transformation in its physical state from solid matter through to gas as air in the atmosphere. Both types of chi mix intensely in the process, especially as vertical chi is redirected sideways by vegetation on the planet's surface. The chakras become internal powerhouses of living energy, activated by a strong, combined flow of chi entering your body from the earth and universe. It is vital that your Crown and Sex Chakras are kept open to freely take up this chi, which then needs to filter through all the chakras. If one of them becomes blocked, this will restrict the flow of energy to the others. If your Stomach Chakra becomes tight, for example, perhaps because you're feeling nervous or stressed, the flow of chi from the earth to the Heart, Throat, Midbrain, and Crown Chakras above will be greatly reduced while the lower chakras become starved of chi from the universe.

WAYS OF REDIRECTING AND REDISTRIBUTING CHI

Use palm healing, similar to reiki, to calm chi in an overactive chakra, or to help close it down so that energy is not drained away too quickly. Firmly place your hands over each chakra to contain chi without letting it dissipate. Sound helps to open up the chakras and accelerates the flow of chi. Chanting will create strong vibrations inside your body; sound waves will surge

MEDITATION AND BREATHING

Sit or kneel with a straight back and focus your mind on each chakra, one at a time. Use separate visualizations to help open, close, activate, or calm the chi contained in each one. Start by breathing chi into the chakra you want to work on and use your mind to alter the energy it contains.

To open up a chakra Think about a yellow daffodil or a tulip unfurling. Visualize drops of water falling into the chakra, sending out ripples or splashing out in all directions. Alternately, imagine the sun rising inside the chakra, spreading light and warmth. Breathe out forcefully to spread your chi out further.

To close up a chakra Envisage the sun setting and spreading a pink glow as your energy levels settle down, or "create" a little creature inside your chakra that curls up and falls asleep. Breathe slowly and deeply in a calming rhythm.

To activate a chakra Imagine a roaring fire at its center, generating a local sensation of abundant heat and energy. Wherever you want some extra chi, picture huge waves rolling up through your chakras before crashing down. Breathe deeply and a little quicker to aid this energizing process.

To calm the chi within a chakra Picture turbulent waters becoming calm and flat. Visualize large snowflakes falling on a soft landscape. Feel the energy coming down. Take long, slow breaths, letting your out-breath trail off slowly before breathing in again.

through your chakras to stir up the energy flow that activates them. Alter the pitch of your chanting to direct the sound to a specific body part (see pages 148-149).

If you want to move chi up through the body, start at the Sex Chakra and work your way up; if you want to lower the chi, start with the Crown Chakra and work your way down. Different meditation and breathing techniques help control the mechanism of the chakras and encourage chi to either become calmer or more active. Combine chanting, meditation, and breathing exercises to open and activate, or close and calm specific chakras. Also use different types of food to help make long-term changes to the way that chi moves through the chakras.

PALM HEALING

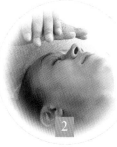

1 Ask your partner to lie on his/her back. Sit with his/her head between your knees. Place your hands over your partner's Crown Chakra at the top of his/her head. Breathe chi, moving your hands away from time to time to feel the chi between your hands and the chakra.

2 Place one hand over the Midbrain Chakra and the other over the initial hand in a "cross." Breathe chi as you make gentle contact. Remain calm to transmit peaceful, relaxed energy. If the palms of your hands become hot when you move them away, this indicates a strong exchange of chi. Continue for as long as you feel changes taking place.

3 Gently place your hands just above your partner's neck or the Throat Chakra. Transmit chi into this area.

4 Rest your hands on the center of your partner's chest to calm

CALIBRATING THE CHAKRAS

Think of the chakras as valves which regulate the different types of chi required to carry out specific activities. If you want more chi in your Midbrain Chakra to solve problems, for example, the Crown Chakra needs to be opened up further to receive more chi from the universe, and the Throat Chakra slightly closed to stop this chi from draining away too quickly. You can open or close, activate or calm, the seven chakras to create certain balances of different types of chi in the body. Adjust your chakras in terms of how much chi they let through, so that all are working in harmony with each other. The five chakras between the crown and sex points take in horizontal-moving chi, enabling the Heart Chakra to absorb the chi directed through it and increase the energy here. Learn to redirect and redistribute chi in such a way that benefits your emotions and how you move through life.

the Heart Chakra. Press more firmly, but only on the out-breath, remembering to relax contact on your partner's in-breath.

5 Slide your hands down to the point where the breastplate

ends and the solar plexus begins at the Stomach Chakra. Start to channel chi into it.

6 Halfway between the rib bones and the navel is the Abdomen Chakra. Rest your hands on it before you begin to send chi. Place the center of your palms just below your partner's navel. Don't push too hard or make sudden, jerky movements.

7 Bring your hands down to the pubic bone. Rest your hands

here before projecting chi into the Sex Chakra. If you don't want to make direct contact with this area, hover your hand above it. You can also try the whole palm-healing sequence on yourself following steps 1-7.

CHANTING

It is my belief that chanting is best done in relatively open, uncluttered surroundings, which help open and expand your outer chi energy field. When you do these exercises, either kneel or sit cross-legged on the floor or in a chair, keeping your back straight, with all your chakras lined up, so chi can flow vertically unhindered. To straighten your lower back, pull back your lower ribs and keep your shoulders still. Tuck in your chin and raise your head as though the crown were being pulled up toward the sky.

Take in long breaths to produce powerful, drawn-out sounds that strongly project vibrations into each chakra. Breathe into each one as you work on it in turn. This is easy to do for the Heart, Stomach, and Abdomen Chakras, but more difficult with the sex point, which needs to be reached by pushing air as far down as possible into the pubic bone. To activate the Crown Chakra, quickly breathe in through your nose to give the incoming air enough momentum so it feels like it is being projected to the top of your head with force. Similarly, breathe in and direct the air into your lower forehead. Constrict your throat and feel the air rushing through your Throat Chakra.

I've found that the lower the pitch of the sound you produce, the further down in your body you will feel the vibration. Begin with a very high-pitched "mmm" sound. If it is high enough, you will feel a slight vibration or tingling sensation at the top of your head. This signifies the opening up of your Crown Chakra as it begins to take in more chi from the universe. If you do this effectively, I guarantee you will feel inspired to use your imagination to produce mind-expanding ideas. As you continue to make the "mmm" sound, lower the pitch a little. Feel the vibration in your lower forehead activating the Midbrain Chakra. This clears the mind, makes thinking easier, and is ideal when you feel mentally dull, lacking in ideas, or need greater clarity. Let the pitch of your "mmm" sound drop much further until you feel a strong vibration in the Throat Chakra. Opening up the energy in here will facilitate the flow of chi between the heart and the mind—important for communication, especially if you want to convey your thoughts with passion.

Try making an "ooo" sound. Vary the pitch until you feel the vibration within the

Heart Chakra in your chest. Sense it radiating out through your breastbone and into your ribs to spread out your emotional chi. Use this sensation to release past upsets, get in touch with your feelings, and open up the Heart Chakra further. Lower the pitch of your "ooo" sound until you feel it vibrating in your solar plexus, where the sound will stimulate the Stomach Chakra. It is relatively easy for chi to become confined here, restricting the flow of energy to the other chakras. If you easily get stressed, focus your chanting on this point to free up the whole channel from blockages. Stimulating this local chi will make it easier for you to develop the necessary power and drive to tackle life head-on.

Utter an "aah" sound and move the vibration further down the body. Adjust the pitch to feel it vibrating around your navel area where the Abdomen Chakra lies. As there are no bones in this area, you may find it harder to feel the same buzz that you get from vibrating your chest, for example, so you will need to make a stronger sound to release more chi and increase vitality. This will help get rid of your fears to give you a more positive outlook. Getting the vibrations to reach down into your sex organs can be challenging. You need to produce an incredibly low, soft "aah" sound similar to a low base note. Breathe in as deep into your body as you can, letting the sound come from the bottom of your throat. Strive to get the pitch low enough to reach the base of your spine. This will help stir up chi around your sexual organs, making it easier to receive and expel chi from here. As you stimulate the sexual chi of this chakra, you will be taking in more energy from the earth. Let it fill your body with the primal force that feeds our most basic instincts for reproduction and survival.

To move chi up through your body, take in a deep breath. Start with the lowest "aah" sound you can muster. Move the vibration up through your body by going into a higher-pitched "aah" sound, then up through a range of "ooo" and "mmm" sounds until you reach to the top of your head—all in one single breath! If you repeat this exercise several times, you will feel your energy levels lift, characterized by a rush of chi into your head. Do this when you feel low and in need of inspiration.

To bring chi down through your body, take in a large breath and work through increasingly lower "mmm," "ooo," and "aah" sounds. The vibration should start from the top of your head and reach as far down as possible. This exercise will prove calming when you are feeling hyper or overemotional. Repeat several times.

BETTER SEX BY CHANNELING CHI THROUGH THE CHAKRAS

PEOPLE

As human emotions, a sense of community, and an awareness of consciousness evolved within our species, sex came to represent more than a simple biological function. Over the ages, it has been refined into a sublime source of pleasure and has become an intimate way to express love and desire. Sex remains a key component of human evolution and, while it is not easy to transcend primal instincts, they can be blended with higher emotional and spiritual energy to provide an experience deeply fulfilling at all levels.

Sex and hunger are the greatest motivational forces in healthy individuals. Like eating, sexual activity is a basic life instinct. The survival of any species depends on the ability to successfully reproduce and sustain nourishment for growth and repair. Evolution has programmed sex into our physical and psychological make up as a primeval necessity. However, the roles of men and women in this process are fundamentally different, opposite yet complimentary to each other.

In my opinion, a good sexual bond encourages a harmonious flow of chi that then acts as a healing energy smoothing over differences and increasing both participants' willingness to connect. As society's approach to sex has become increasingly liberal and candid, people have developed a greater awareness of what for them would constitute a satisfying intimate life.

SETTING THE SCENE FOR SEDUCTION

A bedroom with sexual appeal needs to have enough space for you to exercise complete freedom of expression. If you want to explore other areas of the room during love-making, it helps to have large cushions, or a comfortable armchair, in addition to the bed.

Lighting sets the scene. If you find visual stimuli most enticing, and you enjoy seeing your partner, very dim lights might not work as well as soft illumination. Candles are popular because they add fiery passionate energy to a room. If you both thrive on tactile sensation, being close in a darker room will heighten the experience. Make the

bedroom soundproof enough for you both to feel relatively uninhibited about the sounds you make during sex.

To create a more arousing atmosphere, bring sexual imagery into this intimate space in the form of sculptures, paintings, or photographs of couples together. Strongly scented flowers by your bed can help to heighten the mood. Try orchids as they give off a heady, aphrodisiac scent.

To comprehend how sex functions on a higher level, consider how your chi reacts during intimacy to better understand why you feel sexually aroused, explore what gives you pleasure, and obtain satisfaction. Sexual fulfilment works through reciprocity. Men and women have different demands and each person will require specific stimuli to achieve sexual gratification. In single-sex relationships, for instance, it is easier to relate to your lover's needs because fundamentally you share the same type of sexual energy.

During penetrative sex, your chi interacts very strongly with that of your lover as one partner is literally inside the other. This is when your chi energies mix actively and, if you are open and emotionally charged, you will take in your lover's chi. This process can be so powerful that couples with an active and passionate sex life overcome differences more easily than their less active counterparts. When sexual activity starts to wane, a lot more "problems" come to the fore as differences between each person's chi become more obvious.

You can enhance the intimacy process by activating the chi in your chakras during sex—experiment with moving energy up through the chakras in the male body and down, one at a time, in the female body. Priming and charging the chakras during sex leads to a healthy vitality that allows chi to move swiftly through your body as you reach sexual highs and, ultimately, orgasm. Although this pattern generally differs for men and women, it provides important clues for making both yourself and your lover reach heightened sexual ecstasy. Regular, satisfying sex is the result of an established harmony between your chakras through the active exchange of chi. If your sexual pattern becomes too mechanical, you can miss out on the opportunity to charge the chi of the higher chakras.

To achieve sexual enlightenment, focus on what happens before, during, and after sex. Having understood how the process from arousal to orgasm works, practice and build on your own real-life experience. During love-making, the seven charged chakras in the body map the trajectory of your emotional energy. Use it to explore ways of gaining deeper emotions and pleasures and learn to customize a combination of emotional and sexual energies to suit your needs.

HIGHER PASSION
During sex, it is easy to switch from basic instincts to elevated emotions. Uniting them brings heightened pleasure and excitement to the whole experience.

THE CROWN CHAKRA (SAHASRARA)

Situated at the top of your head, the Crown Chakra allows chi to enter the body and represents your link with the heavens and the spiritual world. It becomes highly active, predominantly during female orgasm. To open up this chakra during sexual activity, breathe in and as low down into your abdomen as possible, then exhale to push your chi high up into your head. Generate momentum as you move energy up into your body on the out-breath. This is where sex and spirituality merge, from the base primal sexual energy of the Sex Chakra to the heavenly chi from your Crown Chakra.

THE MIDBRAIN CHAKRA (AJJNA)

Positioned between the arch of your eyebrows, the Midbrain Chakra is associated with your intellect and will be active in males at the beginning of, and during, sex. It is particularly energetic when males fantasize about sex or are exposed to something arousing. Stimulate the Midbrain Chakra by keeping the lights on, making love by candlelight or in front of a mirror. Imagery and setting are very important for stimulating the Midbrain Chakra as this is where the imagination for inventing and trying out new ways to have sex comes from.

THE THROAT CHAKRA (VISHUDDHI)

Situated in your neck, the Throat Chakra is associated with communication. Stimulate it through kissing or with any sexual activity that uses the tongue. The Throat Chakra acts as a release for energy moving up through the chakras and helps shed light on why women sometimes feel the need to scream out when they orgasm to release some of the energy rushing up into the Crown Chakra. This sensation is often one of tingling. The Throat Chakra may also be activated by talking during sex or verbalizing your fantasies. The sounds made during sex can also be highly stimulating and help you to bond closely by sending out vibrations of chi through the air, harmonizing both partners' outer energy fields.

THE HEART CHAKRA (ANHATA)

Located in the middle of your chest, the Heart Chakra contains the emotional energy of feelings such as love, joy, and intimacy, which can radiate both up and down the body. Through it, an individual decides whether to have sex at all. Stimulate the nipples during sex to increase this local energy. The Heart Chakra acts as a gateway restricting the flow of chi from the lower chakras into the higher ones and vice versa. It might be half-closed when the idea of having sex appeals, but there is no physical urge, or your mind simply says "no." Massage each other's chest to open up the chi contained here.

THE STOMACH CHAKRA (NABHI)

Halfway between the Heart Chakra and your navel, the Stomach Chakra is associated with your drive in life and affects your sexual potency and stamina. When you are feeling very aroused, you may sense a buzz in this chakra and feel a nervous energy from the outset as you begin to engage in foreplay. It can be reassuring to kiss and place your hand over it to contain and nourish the chi there. Too much cold liquid or cold food can dampen down the chi in the Stomach Chakra making it harder to enjoy energetic and long-lasting sex.

THE ABDOMEN CHAKRA (MOOLADHARA)

The seat of your chi, the Abdominal Chakra lies just below your navel. Sexual energy stems from this part of your body and energizing this chakra will encourage a greater appetite for sex and for life in general. You might find that you can precipitate an orgasm simply by breathing deeply into your lower abdomen. In males, this stimulates the prostate gland. During sex, many movements stem from the Abdominal Chakra. If you feel tired or weak in this area, you will lose the stamina and physical strength required to perform at an optimum sexual level.

THE SEX CHAKRA (SWADISTHAN)

The penis and vagina mark the location of the Sex Chakra (linked to primal reproductive needs). As this energy rises, it influences the chi in the other chakras. Increase this flow by moving chi down through the higher chakras or by directly stimulating the chi in your Sex Chakra. Males are easier to stimulate here, whereas females require a stronger energy flow from the higher chakras. The vagina accepts energy, while the penis and testicles expel it, making the male orgasm stronger in the lower half of the body and the female orgasm stronger higher up the chakras.

EATING TO NOURISH YOUR SOUL

FOOD

Your diet helps you determine the quantity and type of chi that you take in through food. Not only is the energy content of it important, but so is the way in which it is eaten. Depending on how ingredients are prepared and later ingested, you can exert changes to the chi content of how and what you eat. Use the energy contained in different recipes to nourish and feed your inner chi, which you can think of as your "soul." Foodstuffs and their respective chi components will penetrate deeply into your central chi channel as they pass through the Throat, Heart, Stomach, and Abdominal chakras. If you fast and bypass the supply of chi normally obtained through food and eating, your body will compensate by absorbing more outer chi through breathing and your surroundings. Yogis, who are masters of this technique, are able to take in the necessary chi for extended periods of time without the assistance of food or eating.

When buying groceries, consider the chi content of your shopping cart. Select edibles that are still "alive"—whole grains, beans, nuts, seeds, vegetables, and fruits—and look for ingredients with strong chi. For example,

HOME TRUTHS

In the company of friends, simply having a good time will fill you up with nourishing chi. During mealtimes in close-knit families, food going around the table is also "blessed" with positive chi that your body can absorb.

SETTING THE SCENE AT MEALTIMES

Every effort should be put into making your designated eating area as peaceful and as relaxing as possible—preferably somewhere spacious, decorated with natural materials, and exposed to fresh air and sunlight. The best type of dining furniture to help you focus on what you are about to eat are straight-backed chairs or stools. They line up your chakras and your central chi channel in a vertical position that facilitates the flow of energy into your body as you eat. Before you sit down to a meal, prepare yourself to receive and assimilate new chi into your system. Sit still and slowly breathe in and out. Try emptying your mind by pondering on the Chinese principle of "one grain, 10,000 grains"—the capacity of a single grain of rice to reproduce thousands (even millions) of other grains.

Conjure up gratitude and appreciation for what you are about to receive by taking time to consider how each type of ingredient was grown and harvested.

Chew every mouthful carefully and break your food down thoroughly. Aim for 30-70 chews per morsel. Avoid drinking at mealtimes as liquids accompanying meals tend to dilute the gastric juices, prolonging digestion. Have a drink at least 30 minutes before or after a meal. Leave a gap of at least half an hour between sweet and savory foods because your digestive system will process desserts more quickly. If there is slower-moving food ahead, this will create conflict in your digestive tract. Once you have finished eating, an additional rush of blood will enter your small intestine (Abdominal Chakra) so let this process run its course before getting on with your day. Allow for the proper digestion of food to assimilate new chi.

choose spindly, knotted carrots that have had to grow in rocky conditions and bend their way around obstacles in the soil over their fat, straight counterparts. When storing ingredients at home, keep them somewhere where there is plenty of fresh, healthy chi—ideally a cool, dry room with exposure to fresh air. As most food comes sealed in plastic wrapping, remove this layer so ingredients can "breathe" and immediately take in the chi of your kitchen or larder. Paper bags allow food to retain its natural chi content and therefore make the best type of storage container.

When preparing meals, avoid electric ranges (and microwaves in particular) because their intense electromagnetic activity disturbs the chi contained in food. As you dish up recipes, some of your own chi will filter into the serving dishes themselves, so it is important that you project beneficial chi as you handle food if you are to transmit positive energy to it. When setting the table, use china or pottery dishes and cutlery that incorporates natural materials like wooden handles.

FASTING TO REPLENISH CHI

Fasting involves trusting in the conviction that you can break the basic connection you have with food and nourish your soul by abstaining from it. This stance will then enable you to draw on other sources to replenish your chi and a different kind of energy will start to pervade your body. As you begin to take in more chi from the universe and planet Earth, you will experience absolute mental clarity, a cleansing of all negative emotions, and a renewed perspective on life.

Decide on the length of your fast. Three days is the maximum duration for most people. Dawn to dusk is very common and a good start. Alternatively, either carry this pattern over for several days, or restrict your food intake to a simple evening meal for a number of consecutive days. If you are considering doing a longer fast, attempt this with the help of someone you can trust. Some individuals experience a high from going without food, so you need someone who can pull you out of this mindset. When you come off the fast, you need to return to the real world and find ways of

FINDING THE RIGHT FAST

Here are my suggestions for different kinds of fast, with a description of their benefits. Fasting will bring about changes to your blood sugar levels and other blood chemistry components. If you have suffered from nutritional deficiencies, diabetes, high or low blood pressure, consult your doctor before attempting any of these fasts.

ONE-DAY FAST

This fast is ideal during the weekend when you can suspend your normal weekday routine. Take in only water for one single day. This brief, rigorous spell of abstinence will give your whole digestive system a welcome rest. You will feel more in charge of what you eat rather than being a slave to your cravings.

DAWN-TO-DUSK FAST

During this fast, drink fluids throughout the whole day, followed by a simple evening meal. In the evening, eat simple, unprocessed foods, such as brown rice, millet, corn on the cob, fresh vegetables, dried beans, nuts, seeds, and fruit.

Follow the ideas covered in Food for Clarity of Thought (see pages 56-63) to bring different chi into your body, break up unhealthy eating patterns, and reset your body's digestion to a new rhythm. Try to sustain this change.

incorporating your abstemious experience into your daily functional routine. Slowly return to your habitual foods, gradually increasing their quantities until you resume your normal eating pattern. Fasting and then bingeing is more harmful than not fasting at all!

In the days before fasting, eat less and follow a more wholesome diet. Take at least two days to ease into your period of abstinence and a further two to come out of it. All fasts allow for an unlimited supply of water, but could also include vegetable juices, fruit juices, and soups. If you include solids, be sure to eat alone or with someone else doing the same fast. Chew every morsel—you will be astonished by the small amounts needed to feel full. Ensure you never get dehydrated; it is better to have too much, rather than too little, to drink. Vegetables, cooked grains, and fruits contain large amounts of liquid; if you exclude any of these ingredients from your diet, replace them with water. Avoid all processed foods and only eat whole grains, beans, and vegetables, gradually reducing the quantities eaten.

THREE-DAY FAST

During this fast, drink only water, herbal teas, or juices for a period of up to three days. Proceed with care and stop if you feel dizzy, shaky, weak, or become exceedingly pale at any time. Avoid if you are anemic, hypoglycemic, or prone to fainting spells. Do not attempt this fast twice in a row without having a break in between sessions.

You should notice a gradual and healthy drop in weight after the first few days. As toxins are eliminated, you could feel very intense emotions. By the third day, you will be more energetic, centered, in harmony with the world. Established eating patterns, emotions, and routines will all gradually fade as your chi becomes purer, "emptier," and you are more receptive to new thoughts, life directions, and changes.

When you come off the fast, those cups of coffee mid-morning or afternoon, or snacks during the day, will be a thing of the past.

10-DAY FAST

This fast consists only of meals of whole grains and vegetables, supplemented by water, juice, tea, and clear vegetable-stock soups. You are allowed three daily meals in the quantities that you desire so long as you chew your food well. For instance, you could have a large bowl of porridge for breakfast; corn on the cob and vegetables for lunch; and brown rice with vegetables for dinner. Use a variety of vegetables and grains; mix brown rice, for example, with whole wheat, rye, or barley.

Initially, you will notice gradual but sustained weight loss. If you adhere to a longer detoxification period, you will start to feel more connected with the universe as you obtain new, interesting insights about yourself and the world. Give yourself 1-2 days to readjust.

INDEX

A

Abdomen Chakra 20, 29, 45, 144-149, 153
acupressure 22, 27, 30, 40, 68, 70-71
 points 59, 97, 118-121
acupuncture 22
ambition 29
anger 47
anxiety 47
apple kuzu 87
asanas 20
auras, seeing and interpreting 78

B

bedroom 150
bells and gongs 74
body alignment 23, 66
body scrubbing 104-107
breathing 20, 26, 28, 38, 50, 54, 145

C

camomile tea 87
candle(s) 74, 76, 139, 150
 meditation 77
ceilings 84
chakras 26, 29, 79, 140
 Abdomen Chakra 20, 29, 45, 144-149, 153
 calibration 20, 146
 Crown Chakra 20, 29, 44, 93, 144-149, 152
 fine-tuning 144-149
 Heart Chakra 20, 29, 45,144-149, 153
 locating 44-45
 Midbrain Chakra 20, 29, 44, 144-149, 152
 seven 20, 144, 152-153
 and sex 150-153
 Sex Chakra 20, 29, 45, 144-149, 153
 Stomach Chakra 20, 29, 45, 79, 144-149, 153
 Throat Chakra 20, 29, 79, 45, 93, 144-149, 152
 visualization 93-95
chanting 148-149
chi energy
 ascending/descending 19
 bi-directional 26
 body 10, 92-127
 body and mind 14, 92-95
 compressed/dispersed 19
 drawing inward 53
 Earth's 36, 144
 emotions 11, 130-153
 energy principles 8
 expanding outward 53
 external forces 9
 fast/slow 19
 food 15, 26, 29, 33, 56-61, 98-100, 138, 154-157
 generating 32
 living space 23
 meditation exercises 33
 mental manipulation of 50
 mind 10
 moving down 52
 moving up 52
 others 27, 31, 34, 46
 outward/inward 19
 personal 18
 redirecting 145
 relationships 15, 136-139
 releasing from head 93
 sex 15, 150-153
 sleep 23, 82, 84-86
 spreading through the head 93
 stabilizing your chi before sleep 88
 therapies 20
 types of 19
 vitality and mental clarity 14
 see also meridians
chi gong 24, 33, 122-125
circulation 38
cleansing rituals 74
clothing 33, 108-111
colors 26, 85, 108-111
communication 29
compass, points of 80
compressed/dispersed energy 19
cooking methods 29
cupping 126-127

D

depression 47
detoxification 56
divination 12
dreams 54, 84, 86

E

Eight Directions 81
elasticity test 11
electromagnetic fields 85
emotions 11, 14, 29, 47
energizing breathing 28
environment (personal) 27, 31, 72-75
envy 47
exercises
 accessing inner chi 32
 body alignment 66-67
 chi moving 50
 cleansing the mind 79
 feeling another's chi 34, 47-47
 feeling Earth's chi 36
 first thought of the day 54-55
 meditation 46, 76
 moving chi 52-53
 seeing and interpreting auras 78
 stimulating acupressure points on your head 68
 visualization 46
 see also acupressure, chi gong, t'ai chi, reiki

F

fabrics 111
fast/slow energy 19
fasting 156-157
fats, saturated 57
fear 47
feet, soaking 86
feng shui 23, 80-85, 138
 color wheel 110
 elements 24
food 15, 26, 29, 33, 56-61, 98-100, 138, 154-157
 see also recipes
fruit 58
frustration 47
full breathing 28
furnishings 85

G

Gall Bladder meridian 132

H

head scrubbing 106-107
headache 51
Heart Chakra 20, 29, 45,144-149, 153
heart chi 47
Heart Governor meridian 131
Heart meridian 133
hysteria 47

I

intellect 29

J

jealousy 47
joints, manipulating 39

K

ki see also chi energy
kidney chi 47
kinesiology 12, 42
Kirlian photography 18
Kirlian, Semyon 18

L

lactic acid 39
Large Intestine meridian 131
Law of the Five Elements 24
lemon tea 65
liver chi 47
Lung meridian 132
lungs chi 47

M

macrobiotics 100
mass consciousness 9
massage see also shiatsu
meditation 26, 28, 32, 46, 54, 76, 86, 88, 92-93, 145
  exercises 33
  tasks 13
menus 60
meridian(s) 68, 140, 144
  Gall Bladder 132
  Heart 133
  Heart Governor 131
  Large Intestine 131
  Lung 132
  Small Intestine 133
  stretches 33, 54, 130
  Triple Heater 130
  see also acupressure
Midbrain Chakra 20, 29, 44, 144-149, 152
minerals 57
mirrors 85
moxibustion 22, 27, 30, 96-97
muscle(s)

relaxing 38, 66
stretching 54
testing 42

N

nutrients, positive and negative 57

O

orientation
  for sitting 83
  for sleeping 82
outward/inward energy 19

P

palm healing 146-147
parsley tea 65
partner, ideal 137
pendulum, using 44
personal aura 18
plants' chi energy 85
prana see also chi energy
professional practitioners 21

Q

qi see also chi energy

R

recipes
  bancha twig tea 103
  blanched salad with vinegar 63
  burdock and carrot 102
  Chinese cabbage and sauerkraut roll 103
  cucumber, Chinese cabbage, and radish salad 62
  green roasted rice tea 103
  hunza apricots with vanilla custard 103
  lentil soup 63
  miso soup 62

noodles 63
pickled radishes 102
polenta with syrup 62
rice balls 102
rice dream pudding 103
shiitake tea 103
shoyu broth 101
soba spice 62
sweet millet soup 101
vegetable stew 63
watercress and shiitake salad 102
whole oat porridge with raisins and sunflower seeds 63
reiki 23, 25, 140-143
  practicing 142-143
relationships 15, 136-139
  see also sex

S

sex 15, 150-153
  sexuality 29
Sex Chakra 20, 29, 45, 144-149, 153
shiatsu 22, 38
  giving a 40
shiitake and dried daikon tea 65
sitting, orientation 83
skin
  scrubbing 27, 31, 33, 104-107
  structure of 105
sleep(ing)
  promoting better 84-85
  peacefully 86
  orientation 82
Small Intestine meridian 133
spirituality 29
spleen chi 47
spring cleaning 73
Stomach Chakra 20, 29, 45, 79, 144-149, 153
stress 14

sugars 57
sweet kuzu root tea 65

T

t'ai chi 24, 33, 112-117
  walk 36
Tantric philosophy 20
teas 26, 29, 64-65, 87
Throat Chakra 20, 29, 79, 45, 93, 144-149, 152
Traditional Chinese Medicine (TCM) 27, 104, 127
Triple Heater meridian 130
tsubo(s) 22, 27, 30, 69, 96, 118
  therapy 70-71

U

umeboshi bancha tea 65

V

visualization 26, 28, 32, 46, 51, 76, 86, 92-95
  before sleeping 89
  exercise 79
vitality 14, 29

W

water 29, 64
workspace 75

Y

yoga 20, 33

ACKNOWLEDGMENTS

I wish to thank: Mum for all the love; darling Dragana for the passion, excitement, and fun; my four most precious boys, Christopher, Alexander, Nicholas, and Michael for the exceptional chi they possess; my sister Mel and her tribe, Adam, Angela, Fran, and Georgina; Dragana's family (all seven of them!)

My friends and colleagues: Jeremy, Boy George, Michael Maloney, Hans and Paola, Karin, Dule, and Enno —it's been great to exchange a part of my life with you! And, of course, the superb staff at "Y," especially Pearl and Greg! And my long-term publishing chums at Carroll & Brown—Denise, Amy, Anna, Emily, Jules, and the staff—it is a pleasure working with you. I mean it!

CONTACT DETAILS

Simon G. Brown, PO Box 10453, London, NW3 4WD
Tel: +44 (0) 20 7431 9897 Fax: +44 (0) 20 7431 9897
Email: simon@chienergy.co.uk
Website: www.chienergy.co.uk

CARROLL & BROWN WOULD LIKE TO THANK

Production Karol Davies, Nigel Reed
IT Paul Stradling, Nicky Rein
Photographic assistance David Yems
Picture Research Sandra Schneider
Index Madeline Weston

PHOTOGRAPHIC CREDITS

p. 18 (top left) Manfred Kage/Science Photo Library; p. 21 *Journal für die Frau*/Camera Press; p. 25 (center) Gary Compton/Camera Press; p. 55 Getty Images.
Front jacket (center left): *Journal für die Frau*/Camera Press.

BIOGRAPHY

Simon Brown certified as a design engineer having two inventions patented in his name. He began studies in Oriental medicine in 1981 and further studied under Michio and Aveline Kushi, Shizuko Yamamoto, and Denny Waxman in the USA before qualifying as a shiatsu therapist and macrobiotic consultant. Simon Brown was director of London's Community Health Foundation for seven years, a charity which ran a range of courses in the Oriental healing arts. Since 1993, Simon has made feng shui and shiatsu his full-time career with celebrity clients like Boy George and large corporations, including The Body Shop and British Airways. Simon is a member of the Feng Shui Society and the Shiatsu Society.

CONSULTATIONS AND COURSES

Simon provides a complete feng shui and healing consultation service. His feng shui consultations can be arranged to include a site visit, or be completed by post, and cover floor plans with the necessary feng shui recommendations with explanations; a full report and a survey; feng shui astrological information for the next four years; the best directions for the current year; and the best dates to implement his recommendations. Ongoing advice by telephone or email is available. Simon also provides shiatsu treatments from his London clinic.

Simon offers a variety of feng shui courses, ranging from one-day introductions to full certificate courses with homework and assessments. He also runs courses for architects and designers.

BOOKS BY SIMON G. BROWN

Simon Brown is the well-known author of the best-selling *Practical Feng Shui* (750,000 copies).

Practical Feng Shui Published by Cassell & Co
ISBN 0-7063-7634-X
Practical Feng Shui for Business Published by Ward Lock
ISBN 0-7063-7768-0
Practical Astrology by Numbers Published by Carroll & Brown
ISBN 1-903258-61-8
Essential Feng Shui Published by Cassell and Co
ISBN 0-7063-7854-7
Choose Your Food to Change Your Mood (with Steven Saunders)
Published by Carroll & Brown ISBN 1-903258-64-2
Practical Feng Shui Solutions Published by Cassell and Co
ISBN 0-304-35476-7
The Practical Art of Face Reading Published by Carroll & Brown
ISBN 1-903258-08-1
Feng Shui in a Weekend Published by Hamlyn
ISBN 0-600-60378-4
Feng Shui Published by Thorsons
ISBN 0-00-719337-9
Feng Shui for Wimps Published by Sterling
ISBN 1-402-70376-7
Energy Booster Workout Published by Newleaf
ISBN 0-7171-3639-6